Speed Train Your Own Retriever

Speed Train
Your Own Retriever

*The quick, efficient, proven system
for training a finished dog*

Larry Mueller

Stackpole Books

Copyright © 1987 by Stackpole Books

Published by
STACKPOLE BOOKS
Cameron and Kelker Streets
P.O. Box 1831
Harrisburg, PA 17105

10   9   8   7   6   5   4

Photographs by Micky Mueller and Ann Cicero.

Printed in the United States of America

Library of Congress Cataloging-in-Publication Data

Mueller, Larry.
    Speed train your own retriever.

    1. Retrievers—Training.   I. Title.
SF429.R4M84   1987   636.7′52   86-23109
ISBN 0-8117-2201-5

To my wife, Micky, who, early in our marriage once said, "A *third* dog? One more and you'll have to choose between me and the dogs." I tell everybody that I promptly bought a fourth dog, but she didn't leave. So I acquired a fifth. Then a sixth and a seventh. And still she stayed. But the truth is, her good nature took over, and she still puts up with my dog addiction, plus my usual 6 to 12 dogs.

Contents

Before You Start

The Speed-Train System is designed for today's busy people who want to train their dogs, but have little time for the job. I have selected the methods that work fastest on dogs with the least intrusion on your time. I do not suggest that you will train a finished dog in seven days, or any other such foolishness. I do claim, though, that if you follow these instructions to the letter, you will end up with a finished dog so easily and with so little total time that you'll scarcely realize you've trained a dog. Rather, training your dog will be a little fun time tucked in here and there between other demands on your time.

Professional trainers may scoff at the number of gadgets and props we use, saying, "All this is unnecessary. Just work with the dog until he understands what you want, and you won't need all this junk." They are right, of course, except that training is a pro's full-time job. He may have the time for it that you don't. Most of our Speed-Train tools cost little or nothing; certainly far less than the price of professional training, so don't neglect their use if you want to teach your dog in the shortest time possible. In other words, if you want to shortcut training time, don't shortcut the system.

As you read this book, note that the photographs serve an important function. As is customary, they help explain and clarify the instructions. The photographs are positioned in the text so they illustrate the printed material immediately following. In essence, the text below each picture can be considered the caption, sometimes a long, long caption, for that photo. This placement will put an end to one of the main annoyances of dog training books. Ordinarily, you read the book before you train. At training time, you refer back to the text for specifics, and more often than not, you must wade through pages and pages to find what you want. No more. Locate the appropriate step in the table of contents, then glance at the pictures to swiftly zero in on the training move you need to know more about at that moment.

In case you've wondered about the use of yellow dogs in the photographs of this book, it is not meant to be a reflection of personal preference, nor does it suggest that yellow dogs are superior. Yellow dogs simply photograph better than black dogs which, unless taken very close, tend to look like ink globs on the printed page.

Pups, the eternal promise of the future, come in various colors. We've used mostly yellow in this book because their photos reproduce better on the printed page.

Part I

Preliminary Conditioning

As soon as the pup becomes accustomed to his new surroundings, get him a collar. (Don't buckle it so tightly that you can't get two fingers under it easily. Remember, too, the little fellow is growing rapidly. You'll have to check and loosen the collar frequently.) Attach a yard of cord to the collar. Let him drag it around all day. The pup won't like either collar or cord, but long before the day is over he'll accept it as normal.

Let the pup leash-train on his time, not yours.

The next day, tie the pup to his carrier (or fence if he's in a kennel) for 15 minutes. If he chews the cord, substitute a light chain. He'll fight and complain, but he'll soon settle down. Add 5 more minutes the next day.

When he learns to accept being tethered without a fight, it's no longer necessary to drag the cord around. And presto! He has conditioned *himself* to being leashed. You won't have to go through those annoying and time consuming struggles when using the leash becomes necessary. Walk the pup on leash occasionally, or by the cord, to maintain this conditioning.

This simple cord training is essential to later off-leash control, so do not neglect it.

If your new retriever pup lives in the house, he'll have to be potty trained. The quickest, easiest way is to use a cage or dog carrier. Locate it where you'll want the dog's bed to remain permanently. He'll have to spend most of his hours in that carrier during the early days, but don't feel cruel. Your pup will, in fact, quickly come to regard this cage as his domain, his private quiet place *and* his refuge or safe place. Further (and this is important; get a pen and underline it in red so you won't forget) make sure every member of the family understands that they *must* respect this safe place. Later, when the dog gets into trouble and runs to his refuge, that's the end of it. He's home safe. There will be no further punishment. This is essential for his psychological development at this age. We want a bold, self-confident hunting retriever, not a dog inhibited for life because there is no refuge from wrath. It will not interfere with obedience later.

The reason the cage or carrier works so well in potty training is that dogs will not willingly dirty their own nests. Coupled with good timing on your part, there will be few accidents.

The first few nights, wrap an alarm clock (not electric, of course) in a towel and place it in the cage with the pup. The ticking seems to replace the heartbeat sounds of littermates and mother. The pup feels less alone and cries less through the night.

As soon as you awake in the morning, take the pup outside to the corner of the yard which will be his permanent potty stop. Select a place that is in a direct line from the door and if possible from his carrier. He'll learn much quicker than with a complicated route.

Feed the pup at exactly the same time morning and evening. Supply water at the same time. Soon after eating, the pup will feel the need to relieve itself. Have him outside at the right spot. It won't take long to learn how many minutes elapse between eating and pottying and, therefore, when to let him out. Later, when the dog has learned where to go (they learn this quickly by smell, and dogs hate to break in new potty places) and how to signal you regarding his needs, water can be available constantly. And when the pup matures, he can be fed once a day.

Step 1

Training While You Feed

The food bowl is your first real Speed-Train tool. You'll have to use it from day one, anyway, so let it teach your new pup COME, HEEL, SIT, STAY, and ALL RIGHT. Almost without extra time or effort, your pup will learn his most important vocabulary long before it's time for serious training.

Speed-training COME.

When it's feeding time, call "Duke, COME," (substitute his own name, of course) as you pick up his bowl and walk toward the dog food container. Very quickly, little Duke will be rushing to join you on command.

Speed-training HEEL.

Fill the bowl. Hold it low for Duke to smell on your left side. Say "Duke, HEEL," and still holding the bowl low for him to smell, walk several yards before placing the bowl on the ground or floor. He'll usually follow eagerly. If you get a pup that already loves to roam and investigate more than eat, control him with a leash.

Speed-training SIT.

But don't let Duke eat just yet. Gently hold your right hand against Duke's chest to restrain him. (He's still on your left side.) Press his haunches down as you say "SIT."

Speed-training STAY.

Still holding his haunches down gently, bring your right hand away from his chest and hold it before his face traffic cop-style, as you say "STAY."

After a moment, say "ALL RIGHT," and release him to eat, praising him highly with "Good Boy!" and stroking the length of his back for a few moments as he eats. (The praise and petting will also avoid future confrontations at the food bowl which occur with some dogs.)

Duke won't understand any of this at first, but one day it will click. He'll learn the commands through repetition, and you'll never miss the few extra moments it takes. It's so fast and easy that you and Duke will scarcely realize you're training. And the pup will know his basic commands by the time he's three months old.

Important: There is a natural tendency for a dog to come toward you when its name is called; therefore, we have used Duke's name only with COME and HEEL. SIT and STAY are restraining commands, and ALL RIGHT is permission to leave you, so we do not precede these commands with Duke's name.

Extra important: Dogs are such creatures of habit that if they are taught commands in one place only, they think they're supposed to obey in that one place only. This is not obstinance. It's canine response to circumstances which to them includes the location and our body movements as well as our voice. (In fact, although we regard our words as most important, dogs respond more naturally to our body movements which they often quickly learn to respond to before our words leave the tongue.)

The pup learns fastest in one location, yet we must avoid teaching one-location obedience. The solution to this dilemma is simple. Do the COME-HEEL-SIT-STAY-ALL RIGHT routine in one place until a pattern is established and the pup is performing very well. After that, pick a second location to form a pattern, then a third, fourth, fifth, and sixth. By that time, the pup is understanding that he does this routine anywhere he's asked. After that, to further discourage location obedience, switch to a different one of the six locations at every feeding. If possible, add even more locations.

Super important: This is puppy training, and he *will* learn quickly and easily if you carry out these instructions calmly and persistently. *Never* lose your patience and raise your voice at this time, or you will severely set back the training and cost yourself a *great deal* of extra time overcoming your mistake.

Warning: As much as possible, avoid looking straight at the dog. This is what one dog does to another when it's about to attack, so it's a threatening gesture in dog language.

Step 2

Reward Training and Initial Retrieving

I wager you're amazed at how quickly your pup learned all five commands with the food bowl routine. Keep it up. Dogs retain instruction through repetition. Your pup is just a baby and will forget it all if you stop now. Anyway, it really isn't costing you any time. But you'll want to play with your pup, too. The busiest person in the world can't resist that. Or if he can, he shouldn't own a dog. And because you're playing with the pup anyway, you may as well use selective playing and make it a learning experience. The pup *will* learn from whatever play you engage in (that's what play is all about in dogs and children — practice and preparation for things they will do as adults), so you might as well select play that will speed up, rather than retard, the training process. It won't even cost you any extra time.

This is a fun time no-no.

First off, don't roughhouse. Pups love it, but it teaches bad habits that will cost time correcting later. A feisty pup trying to fight and bite your hand is cute, but an adolescent dog that thinks it has permission to do that is a serious pain, possibly even a threat, or eventual threat, to some child or even an adult.

Instead, use play time to enlarge on what the pup has already learned with the food bowl. Duke now expands his horizons by discovering that the words he already knows bring fun and rewards without the food bowl.

This time our prop is a thinly sliced wiener. Or it can be pieces of gravy bread, or any leftover goodies from dinner — except bones, of course. Small pieces of cooked liver are great. Dogs have individual likes; cater to his. Don't use his ordinary food or dog biscuits. That's not as exciting.

Don't worry if Duke isn't yet responding well to commands at the food bowl. Start the play training anyway. It will only reinforce, or help begin, what we're teaching with the food bowl.

Say "Duke, COME!" (always with the emphasis on the command word, and always with an excitement in your voice — *never* harsh, screaming, or threatening). It's not mealtime, so Duke may be confused and not respond. Don't worry. And *don't* become angry. All this puppy training must be play, not serious and demanding. Otherwise, we'll irreparably inhibit the pup. What we're after is not a finished dog at a record early age, but a pup that already knows basic commands by the time he's ready for serious training. Remember, we're doing this without having to set aside time for training.

Guaranteeing COME.

OK. Duke didn't respond to COME in the new situation. No problem. Say it again. This time squat down to his level at the word COME. This is tremendously inviting for a dog. It's almost guaranteed to bring him running. Praise him lavishly. "Good boy!" Stroke him. And reward him with a slice of wiener or whatever he might like better. And remember this squat ploy for anytime you may need it with the untrained pup—especially when you're in the yard or somewhere and don't have a goodie or the food bowl to offer.

Guaranteed HEEL.

Now that you have his attention, stand, hold a slice of a wiener, or a wiener, in front of his nose, and say "Duke, HEEL," and walk several yards.

Treat-trick SIT.

Now stop, bring the wiener back over Duke's nose as you say "SIT." It's unlikely that he'll back up as the goodie passes over him. Instead, he'll follow it with his nose and sit automatically as his nose goes upward. If he doesn't, use your hand to sit him. Praise him. And give him part of the goodie.

Duke is on your left side as he goes from HEEL to SIT. Always bring him to SIT at your left so it becomes another of Duke's good habits that saves time for you later.

Duke is already learning the restraint of STAY at the food bowl, so as soon as he's responding well to SIT with the goodie, it's time for STAY.

He'll STAY with the treat.

Holding the goodie above Duke's nose with your left hand, command STAY as you bring the right hand toward his face in a traffic cop gesture, and step forward on your *right* leg. (Stepping forward on your left would bring your leg motion right past Duke's eyes, urging him to follow rather than stay.) Hold Duke at STAY just for a moment before giving him his reward of praise and goodie.

As Duke learns the game, you'll be able to move back another step while he holds at STAY. Then gradually another and another before going back to give him the reward. Soon, you'll be able to walk all the way around him and finally at considerable distance. But always return to give Duke the reward. In the future, Duke will be expected to STAY for extended periods. If we break the STAY with the COME command, we'll teach Duke that STAY just means, "Sit for a moment while anxiously waiting to break and run to the boss." That habit, of course, would cost us a bunch of training time to correct in the future. We're speed-training.

At first, this play sequence is COME, reward, HEEL, SIT, reward, STAY, reward. When Duke gets good at it, skip the reward after COME. If, or when, Duke still plays the game as well without the COME reward, skip the reward after SIT, only rewarding after the whole game has ended with STAY.

Over the next two or three months, gradually lengthen Duke's time at HEEL and STAY as well as the distance you walk away during STAY. Form location patterns first, then alternate locations, and finally practice in many different places to reinforce the understanding that commands are obeyed wherever they're given.

At last, forget the goody one time out of five, only rewarding that time with lavish praise. When this is working well, forget the goody one time out of three. Then every other time. If, or when, Duke is responding to the play training *as well with reward as without,* stop the goodies entirely, rewarding only with praise.

The COME-HEEL-SIT-STAY game is fun, of course, but it's not the only game to play with a retriever whose whole entire future is based on his ability to fetch. As soon as Duke is responding somewhat to COME, add FETCH play.

Start the little fellow with a small dummy or one of your socks stuffed with rags. These are light and easy to carry, so they will not promote hardmouth, which would require training time to cure later. Do not throw sticks, engage in tug-of-war games with the pup, or train two pups at once and let them compete for the dummy. All of these promote chewing or hardmouth.

The little dummy or sock will be easy for Duke to find because you won't be able to throw either very far, and they won't bounce around like a rubber ball. The sock has the advantage of naturally carrying your odor. If in doubt, wear it a day. The dummy can be carried a day or wiped with perspiration to add more of your odor than your hands can impart. We won't explain how and why right now, but take it on faith that this is very important. Later on, we'll use your scent in a way that will save you an enormous amount of retraining time when young Duke, for any one of a variety of reasons, loses his confidence.

Allowing bad habits to begin means losing time correcting them. We're Speed-Training, so we won't just throw the dummy and hope Duke will bring it back. Just as likely (if not now, a little later) he'll decide to run around you, trying to tempt you into chasing him to get the dummy back. *Don't yell about it.* No punishment or threat of punishment should be associated with retrieving. Also, position yourself between the pup and his house or cage. When he picks up the dummy, he'll probably head home with his prize. Catch him as he goes by, and he won't require as much urging with the check cord.

Throw the dummy a few feet (always underhanded and right past Duke's eyes), say FETCH as he runs toward the dummy to pick it up, then if necessary, urge, never yank, the dog back toward you with the cord. It won't be a big deal. Remember? We already had Duke condition himself to being tethered, so most of the fight is over, and no time was wasted. Praise the little dog highly as you say GIVE and take the dummy. If Duke doesn't care to give it up, just push it farther back in his mouth. He'll shove it out with his tongue.

A moving dummy has greater attraction.

Duke wasn't interested? He ran out, looked at the dummy, then walked off? OK, tie a cord to the dummy. You'll tangle it with Duke's check cord occasionally, but it won't be much of a problem if you work with short throws. Toss the dummy several feet. This time, when Duke chases the dummy while it's in motion, but loses interest when it stops, give the dummy a jerk with the cord. Duke will probably pounce on it. Urge him in for the delivery.

Some pup's interest can be peaked by dropping a tennis ball. It bounces. He tries to catch it, but he bumps it with a clumsy foot. The ball rolls farther, urging him to chase. Finally he grabs it. Great fun!

If the pup still isn't interested, don't get excited. He's a baby. Keep testing him every two or three days. If he has retrieving instincts, he'll soon be fetching the dummy. If he doesn't show interest by four months of age, talk to the breeder about another pup.

A timely tap for teaching NO.

Play time is also when to teach NO – unless, of course, Duke is a house dog, in which case you'll have ample opportunity to teach that command at an early age when he's caught chewing your shoe or whatever mischief puppies are so adept at getting into. If Duke lives outside, drop an attractive item like an old shoe, a ball of yarn, or a small cardboard box in the area during fetch play. Arm yourself with several feet of bamboo pole or a fishing rod, and go on with the fetch play. When Duke is attracted by the new object, say NO and gently tap him on the nose to discourage him. This not only teaches NO, but instills a certain awe regarding the length of your reach. Eventually, we will convince Duke that your reach extends into infinity, and that disobedience is dangerous at any distance.

Important: All of this puppy play is exactly that – *play!* Don't make it work by overdoing it. Run through play obedience and play fetch for a few minutes each, then quit. Give an enthusiastic pup perhaps six fetches, and one that gets bored easily only two or three. Keep in mind, his attention span is short. It won't hurt to play-train two or three times a day, if you like, but always quit long before the pup becomes bored.

Extra important: Don't make him dread these play sessions by becoming angry. No matter what happens, maintain the excited spirit of play. And be aware that if you're saying sweet things through gritted teeth, the pup will know your true feelings. If a dog trainer doesn't have great patience, he'd better be a great actor.

Super important: As soon as the play-training sessions are over, it's back to the kennel for Duke. Or back inside, if he's a house dog. No more play of any kind. This play-training *is* his play. He'll look forward to this play-training – and later to serious training – if he's never permitted aimless self-play outside the kennel or house. His enthusiasm for your kind of "play" will be enhanced, so you'll always have his attention. This saves an enormous amount of training time.

Step 3

Whistle

Little Duke is just beginning to respond to your voice commands at the food bowl and during play-training. He's learning fast. His mind is open and receptive because you've planted the message that learning what you want and responding quickly brings delightful rewards. Like children, pups don't always get it right. But also like children, they absorb simple languages (voice, body, facial) at a rapid rate.

If you're going to teach whistle commands, now is the time to do it. Too few hunters bother. It seems difficult. So they wait until the pup is "older and smarter." They try it about the time the pup becomes a 15-year-old boy with all the answers, and then it *is* more difficult. They give up. And then Duke never does learn to handle at a distance. If they want him to fetch that long fall, they have to get out of the duck blind and spook incoming flights while they lead Duke to the area he needs to search. If they have a sore throat, they can whisper commands to the winds. If their voice doesn't carry as far as Duke follows a running pheasant, and he suddenly encounters a skunk. . . .Well, you get the picture.

Actually, there's no good reason *not* to whistle train. It takes no additional time. You're already teaching voice commands. All you do is blow the whistle immediately before saying each command. Before long, the pup begins to connect a certain whistle signal with COME. Eager to get his reward, he starts coming to the whistle instead of waiting for COME. From that point, it's just a matter of practicing to establish the whistle signals firmly in the pup's mind so he doesn't forget. We also keep using whistle signals in other training, so Duke simply grows up understanding both whistle and voice commands. We have the capability of using voice commands for close work and when we forget the whistle, and the whistle for reach and authority when needed. Best of all, though, it costs us no extra time.

I like a two-tone whistle. The end with a ball sounds like a police whistle and carries farther. But I don't care for that blast in the ears when the dog is close enough to hear the plain end. An unnecessarily loud whistle is also an intrusion on the peace and quiet of the outdoors.

Whistle signals are easy to teach and carry longer distances with more authority in the field.

You can use any combination of whistle signals you like, just as you can say HERE, or even GIT for COME. The dog doesn't care. But you'll get the job done faster and easier if you use the Speed-Train signals.

COME. Have you heard a covey of bobwhite quail flush? You can mimic the sound by bringing the tip of your tongue to the roof of your mouth just behind your front teeth, then blowing. Your tongue flutters. Now do this as you blow into the plain end of the whistle. It makes a trilling sound. A long trill will be our COME signal.

Why? Suppose you chose one blast for COME. Or even two. What happens if the dog doesn't respond instantly? There's no room for tolerance. You can't keep repeating the command, or the dog learns that obedience can wait. So you must punish. The more you punish, the more you erode rapport, and the more your dog becomes mechanical in response.

On the other hand, the long trill sounds very insistent. And it can be continued until the dog responds. There's no need for punishment unless the dog simply ignores you.

Right now, of course, we won't be punishing at all. This is still puppy play. And there's really no need for punishment because the pup already knows COME, and he hurries to get the reward. We're just adding the long trill before the voice command.

If there are days when the pup doesn't care to play, don't get excited. No play, no wiener slices. Forget it. If Duke doesn't come when called to his food bowl, postpone his dinner. Try again later. Eventually, he'll get hungry and cooperate.

SIT. There is no whistle for HEEL. It's unnecessary. The dog is always close enough for that voice command. But after heeling, blow one sharp authoritative blast immediately before ordering SIT. For now, the dog will always be right beside you when the SIT command is given, so there's no need for a continuing signal. If the pup doesn't sit even after the verbal command which follows the whistle blast, press him into a sitting position with your hand. No problem. He'll eventually get the idea, and it will become a habit. When the dog is older, and it's necessary to sit him at a distance by whistle, a single blast will do it because practice has made the habit strong by that time.

ALL RIGHT. This verbal command is a release from restraint that means GO to the dog. Right now it means it's OK to leave SIT-STAY and go eat the food in the bowl. Later, the whistle version of ALL RIGHT will precede the FETCH command and even take the place of FETCH, meaning it's OK to go after the dummy. It will also be useful in the field when we're ready to release him, or when perhaps we want him out quartering, and he's loafing at our side. He is accustomed to rushing forward when we say ALL RIGHT, so he does it from habit in this new situation. Or at least he will if we make a fast step forward with him for encouragement. In addition, if we train Duke to handle, we'll have to stop him with the SIT whistle, then give him a new direction with our arm as we blow the whistle for GO.

We begin converting all this to the whistle by blowing a rapid two notes – tweet–tweet – immediately before saying ALL RIGHT at the food bowl. With the food bowl as incentive, little Duke will be amazingly quick in learning to anticipate the voice command and go with the *tweet–tweet.*

That's it! All you've done is feed your dog and play with him. With almost no extra time, you've Speed-Trained him into knowing COME, SIT, and GO in two languages. In the next step, Duke will learn one more whistle signal. But don't worry, it will come as easily and as automatically as did these first three.

Important: When the pup begins responding reliably to the whistle, start mixing it up. Sometimes use just the whistle, sometimes just the voice. Don't always use the whistle and let him forget his first language.

Extra important: Don't stop training when it's evident that Duke knows his whistle signals. Pups forget quickly. Continue with both whistle and voice commands while feeding and playing, and the pup will grow up knowing the commands instead of requiring a great amount of time to relearn them later.

Super important: Your wife doesn't listen to your advice, and your children don't mind, but your dog is beginning to give you a feeling of *power!* He's starting to obey your every whistle, almost like a live robot. If you keep this up, by hunting season, he'll *really* be your willing slave. Be careful. Nothing is more annoying to hunters than the companion who is constantly splitting the air with whistle signals to continually nag at his dog. It brands you as an amateur. While hunting, learn to use the whistle only when necessary.

Bonus: Altogether too few hunters use a dog whistle. Hunters who become genuine dogmen, however, put on a whistle as automatically as their under- wear. Occasionally, a hunter is lost, and search and rescue people have found that a whistle is far more valuable in helping them find you than is the old three–shot SOS from your firearm. In the first place, most hunters use up their ammo before anyone realizes they're lost and starts looking. You can keep blowing the Morse Code short-short-short, long-long-long, short-short-short SOS on the whistle indefinitely. If it gets really bad, and you're in a weakened condition, you can put the whistle in your lips and just breathing through it may make enough noise to alert a trained rescue dog.

Step 4

Quartering or Running a Hunting Pattern

I love to take dogs for walks. The outdoors is a constantly changing face that forever holds me fascinated, and I most love sharing it with a dog. I have less and less time for just enjoying a walk. If I'm going to do it, anyway, I might as well be Speed-Training a pup.

Some pups are bold and race ahead. Others are "boot polishers." If you're strictly a waterfowler, there's no need for ranging ahead. The same applies if you want a non-slip retriever at your side whether hunting waterfowl or upland game. In those cases, use your walks to practice keeping the dog at your side, or at least nearby. Just voicing displeasure every time the pup gets a little too far will control some dogs. Others will require a leash for early control until walking at your side becomes a habit.

If, however, you intend to use your retriever to flush upland game, he will have to run a hunting pattern; that is, he will run a windshield wiper pattern in front of you to search for whatever game might be found and flushed within shotgun range.

Just stand. A little boredom will swiftly teach what you can't.

To begin, take little Duke to a park or other area where grass is fairly short. It's not as tiring as tall foliage. A little pup also will move out more confidently if he can see farther, so it speeds the process of learning to range. If, at first, the pup does not want to leave your side, hurry his training by just stopping. Stand there until Duke becomes bored and starts to run around investigating. Move with him, but stay behind. When he returns to your side, just stand there again. Always keep facing him so he becomes accustomed to being out front. It won't take many short walks before the pup is happily running to the fore.

As the pup grows older and bolder, start to walk a zigzag route. Walk about 50 steps in one direction, then turn and do the same in the other direction. You'll be advancing forward while walking about 25 yards on either side of an imaginary line. That's as wide as you'll want the dog to range because eventually he'll also be about that same distance ahead. Ranging farther would put the game out of range before you had time to shoot, especially if it was flushed at the extreme end of the dog's swing. For Speed-Training purposes, it's smart

Duke may not want to leave your side the first time in the field.

to establish range and running pattern right from the beginning rather than let the dog run wild at first, then waste time modifying his behavior later.

At first, you'll have to walk the whole zigzag route with the pup. Soon, however, the pup will turn, run past you, and be at the 25-yard extreme almost before you get started. Gradually, you'll walk less and less of the zigzag until finally, you can walk a straight line while Duke still runs the hunting pattern.

Teach quartering pattern with whistle for attention and hand and body motion as guides to follow.

Starting with the first time you walk a pattern, use your dog whistle each time you turn to go in the opposite direction. Blow a long, low (not trilling) note. This is not a commanding blast, just a signal to get Duke's attention. It is deliberately long, as in the COME signal, so it can be continued without a conflict, or need for punishment, until the pup looks your way. When he does look up, point with extended arm, and walk in that direction. The pup will follow and no doubt run on past you. Walk along until the pup is about 25 yards from the center line, then whistle and hand signal for another turn.

At first, the pup may think the whistle means COME, but he'll soon know from your body language that it means COME AROUND or TURN. The recognizable difference is that you stand still to receive Duke when you whistle COME. For COME AROUND, you keep on walking.

The check cord demands response to the whistle.

As the pup grows bigger and becomes more confident, he may decide he'd like to run farther to each side than you're allowing. If he starts ignoring the whistle, don't let it become a habit. Immediately begin quartering him on a 50-foot check cord. Blow the whistle just as he reaches the end of the cord. He either turns voluntarily or gets a rude awakening when he hits the end of the cord. With practice, he learns it's not a matter of choice. When the whistle blows, he *must* turn.

Most retrievers are not jug-headed about this, but if yours is, use a choke chain instead of a buckled collar to impart a stronger message when it's time to turn. If this is necessary, see *Step 19* to learn the correct way to put the chain on the dog's neck. (At first glance, you may not realize that there's a right and wrong way to install a choke chain.)

Duke has learned to hunt to the front, quarter, and turn to whistle and hand signals — all accomplished while he's been taken for a walk.

Important: Especially when the dog is first learning to run a hunting pattern, always work into the wind. *Dogs naturally tend to quarter into the wind.* When you finish the course, walk him back at HEEL, or better yet, do land retrieves on the way back to the starting point. *Dogs take straightest lines when running with the wind.* You can repeat quartering the course and fetching back, but don't overdo it. Always quit while it's still fun for both of you.

Step 5

Water

If conditions are right, you can easily have a pup swimming at 12 weeks. Sometimes they swim the first time out. It's nice when they learn early because swimming is something that just comes automatically from then on. *But,* and this is important, starting early is not essential, nor is it wise when conditions are not right.

Temperature is the key to whether the pup acquires an immediate and lifelong love of water or a distasteful first impression that requires much training time to correct. Obviously, because we're Speed-Training, we'll choose the former, regardless how old the pup happens to be when the right time occurs. How the pup takes to water also depends upon his temperament, coat, and heredity. Because these may be unknowns, we'll play it safe.

Water looks solid to an inexperienced pup, and regardless how funny his experience may appear to us, it's a terrible surprise when the pup gallops right out onto this surface that not only isn't solid, but doesn't seem to have a bottom, either. If the water also happens to be cold, the total shock can be enough to make the dog swear off water for life.

Duke's first experience with water is important. Make it shallow.

Begin water introduction by crossing ditches and going through puddles when taking the pup for walks. If the pup only splashes through shallow water, being a little cold won't cause any problems, and water automatically becomes a safe thing in the dog's mind.

Pick a hot day, and he'll like deeper water better.

To introduce deep water, however, choose a hot day—the hotter the better. Take the pup on his walk in the vicinity of a pond or creek, but stay away from it. First, run the pup until he's panting hard and his tongue is hanging from the heat. *Then* take him to the water. Pick a shallow spot, and walk into it yourself. Encourage him to follow.

It's almost certain that little Duke will splash into the water and stand there trying to lap up the lake. The water feels so cool on his hot belly that he may lie down in it or walk out farther. He'll be sopping wet and delightfully cool. One thing for sure, the sensation is so great that Duke develops an instant love affair with water.

Toss the first dummy to the shore's edge, then gradually work out to deeper water.

Don't worry if he's hesitant. Keep quiet.

Give Duke a big welcome when he returns with the dummy.

Make the next throw a little farther out.

Keep stretching his limits, and Duke will soon be swimming for the dummy.

Let him play in the water until he's cool and appears about ready to leave and look for new diversions. Then bring out his dummy. Toss it near the water's edge. Very gradually, toss the dummy farther and farther out until at last the pup's feet no longer touch bottom. He's having fun, and he wants to get that dummy, so chances are he'll do what comes naturally and keep trying to run through the water. If he does, he'll swim, and because it's only for a few feet, he'll hardly notice anything was different.

If Duke is very young, such as 12-to-16 weeks old, don't try to urge him into deeper water and longer retrieves. And don't wear him out. Quit while it's great fun. Take him home and let him think about this wonderful water experience for the rest of the day and through the next. Don't do anything the next day—no walk, no play fetch, no anything. Just let him remember and build up hopes. Then, sure enough, on the following day, his wish is granted. Wow! Water! And he's hooked for life.

A few pups aren't quite so bold and enter this new experience more tentatively. Don't worry about it. Just skip a day as indicated above, and try again. Expose him to water every other day until he develops a love for it. Don't force him, or he'll develop a fear instead.

If the pup is too slow in taking to water, arrange to have another dog along that already loves water. Seeing the other dog having fun will stimulate yours.

Important: When beginning water retrieves, be sure to pick a shoreline where the wind is blowing toward you. If Duke fails to fetch, the wind will return the dummy, anyway. You won't feel the need to become insistent that Duke go after it as you might while watching the dummy drift progressively farther away. *Everything* about water should be a *good* experience.

Equally important: Professional trainers will tell you they don't want to start a pup before he's several months old. That's because they prefer to wait until the dog is old enough to grasp and retain basic training at a rapid rate. They know the owner doesn't want to pay monthly rates while a little pup gradually learns. But the fact that pros don't do it makes many dog owner/trainers think there's something wrong with starting pups early. There isn't. In fact, it gives you the greatest chance to develop your dog's full potential. You're teaching him at a time when he's receptive to learning, so learning-to-learn becomes a pattern for life. You can do what most of us can't afford to have a pro do for us: start the pup right and at the right time. The only danger lies in expecting too much, and becoming angry when you don't get it. If you do this, even a pro may never be able to overcome the inhibitions you've instilled in the dog.

Step 6

Sight of Gun

The shotgun should signal excitement, not fear, so introduce it at fun times.

Develop interest in the gun instead of fear.

At feeding time, when you're ready to go through the COME-HEEL-SIT-STAY-ALL RIGHT routine, grab the shotgun as you say COME and head for the dog food sack or barrel. Duke will be sitting beside you, waiting anxiously, as you dish up his food. Prop the gun against the barrel, wall, or whatever, right beside him. He probably won't even notice it. If you can, carry it along as you go through HEEL, SIT, STAY, and ALL RIGHT. Lay the gun down beside the bowl as he starts to eat. He may notice it after eating, and might sniff its odors, if not the first time, probably before the week is out. Do this for about 10 days. It's not taking extra time, the pup is small, and it's a long while until hunting season, so don't rush it.

Working the shotgun action accustoms the dog to startling noises.

After the 10 days, if you're sure the pup has noticed and examined the gun and regards it as just another object, give Duke his food, but don't place the gun beside it. Walk across the room or, if outside, several yards away, and when Duke is deeply engrossed in eating, work the action of the shotgun. One time. No more.

If it startles Duke enough to stop eating, or to run, don't do it again for three days. After his memory has faded, try it again, but from twice as far.

Chances are, it won't bother him a bit. When you're sure it doesn't, begin the practice of working the action right *before* the whistle signal and calling COME. The shotgun action will soon become another dinner call.

When Duke is coming to the sound of the gun's action, begin working the action one time while he eats. After several days, work the action twice, then three or four times.

If all is going well, let the shotgun action also signal that it's time for a play-training session. By now Duke is probably enthusiastic about the gun, and you'll be able to work the action each time right after throwing the dummy — hopefully, while the dummy is still in the air.

By now, Duke is associating the sight, and one of the sounds, of the shotgun with things he loves most. Don't stop there. He loves to leave the kennel, too. Work the action as he does. Take it along on walks. And work the action during water retrieves.

When you're into several days of accepting the gun during the play-training sessions, and the other times mentioned, you can discontinue working the action at the food bowl.

Important: Don't avoid this just because you own a double instead of an automatic or pump with a noisier action. Either close the double sharply, or use a rifle that has a noisier action. Always use a long gun, however, You don't hunt birds with a pistol.

Extra important: Be reminded that Duke is still quite small. Take him along at his own pace, but don't push him. Don't become angry. And praise *every one* of his successes with convincing enthusiasm. Praise is what makes a dog do it even better next time. We're all suckers for it. Try it on your spouse and kids as well.

Super important: The three parts of Speed-Training are: 1. Choosing the methods which teach dogs with the least investment in time; 2. constantly building on what the dog has already learned; and 3. never letting a problem develop that requires extra time to correct. It's human nature to read instructions and decide, "Oh, I won't need to do that part." Don't shortcut unless you have time to redo what you didn't have time to do right in the first place.

Step 7

More on Commands

Suppose your kids decided to name the little bitch pup Sweet Thing. You figure, what's in a name—a rose is a rose, and all that. Then the pup picks up the word "snuggle" because your little girl says it every time she cuddles the pup. The pup loves cuddling, of course, and comes running every time your little girl suggests they snuggle. You've neglected training somewhat, and here you are in the duck blind. Sweet Thing has wandered off down the shore while you weren't looking. Ducks are on the horizon. And you want that dog back in the blind. Yelling COME doesn't register. You know what will. But can you yell it? Can you imagine yourself out there with buddies, within earshot of two other blinds, and yelling with conviction, "Snuggle, Sweet Thing!"

Maybe that example is a bit exaggerated, but I hope it gives you an idea of why I like to use commands that come to mind naturally, as well as choosing dog names that are appropriate. I don't say BACK when I mean FETCH just because "all the trainers do it." And I don't say KENNEL when I mean GET IN. As I've said before, the dog doesn't care what words you use. You can convince him that STAND means SIT. But why have to convince yourself first?

If the word doesn't arrive on the tongue automatically, you'll have to think each time you use it. You'll even have to train yourself to use it properly. If you don't really believe the word suits the situation, you won't say that word with the same inflection and emphasis that you use with the word that really does apply. Again, it doesn't matter what words you use for commands, just be sure they are the words you believe are appropriate.

Having said that, I'll go back to KENNEL or GET IN. Take your choice, or say something else like LOAD. I like GET because it's a sharper command. IN is unnecessary, but I say it because that's what comes most naturally, and therefore I feel it best adds convincing tone to my command.

Use the hand signal with GET IN, a command which costs almost no extra time to teach.

Any way you say it, GET IN is a handy extra command. And it won't cost you anything—almost none of your time. You're putting the dog in the car, or through the gate, or in the kennel, or through the door and back into the house, or into something else somewhere. Whatever, or wherever it is, take a moment and SIT the dog first. Then motion with your hand, and say GET IN. You might have to grab a collar and help the dog along at first, but not for long. Almost without extra effort you'll have a dog that will sit for inspection and clean-up instead of jumping into the car with muddy feet. And now the dog will get into whatever you say – the boat, the duck blind, and even into the weeds or other cover while hunting.

Start DOWN from SIT, and just show Duke what you want.

This gentle DOWN instruction works faster than more forceful methods because it doesn't meet with the dog's resistance.

Maybe you'd like your dog to learn DOWN so he will lie prone out of the way while in a boat or automobile. Some hunters feel there's no need for DOWN because the ducks don't seem to care if a dog is sitting up. You decide. If you want to add the command to Duke's vocabulary, begin with SIT. With his rump on the ground, he's already half-way down. All that's left is to say DOWN, and gently pull (don't yank and startle him) Duke's front legs out from under him. ATTA BOY him. Pat and praise him for being so smart (even though one hand on the collar may be necessary to hold him down while the other pets) and after some practice, he'll go down on command without you having to pull his front legs.

A wiener treat speeds Duke DOWN even faster.

If Duke is coming along fast, and is still quite young, you may want to add DOWN to the play-train routines. To speed things up, SIT the dog, then hold the wiener slice or other goody near the dog's nose, and move your hand to the ground as you say DOWN. The pup will probably drop right along with the goody. Praise him highly and let him have it. If he doesn't go down by himself, it will be necessary to slip both feet out from under him with one hand as you bring the goody down with the other. Praise and reward as usual. It won't be long before he'll understand.

Use these GET IN and DOWN commands as often as possible as the pup grows up so he doesn't forget them.

Hot item: Is Duke having trouble with a certain command? Here's a great solution I got from Warren, New Jersey animal behaviorist Steve Rafe. Ordinarily, we say ATTA BOY or GOOD BOY to praise a dog that obeys a command. But if the dog is having trouble with that command — really doesn't want to obey it — Steve substitutes the command word for BOY. In other words, it might be GOOD SIT! instead of GOOD BOY! Every time you say it, the praise reinforces the command. Very perceptive. And very effective.

Step 8

Decoys

Just as soon as little Duke is doing well on simple play-training retrieves, it's time to introduce decoys. He's still a little small to lug them, so he can be easily discouraged from fetching them instead of the dummies. In addition, he's used to working close. Also, he's not under the pressure of being steadied (not allowed to go until sent), so a mild correction at this time won't overstress the situation now as adding it later might.

To Speed-Train Duke not to fool with decoys, start fetch practice right in the middle of a stool laid out on the lawn. Stool, of course, means a group of decoys. Scatter several about 10 feet to either side of you.

Duke is on leash or not, depending upon how rowdy and flighty he is at this age. If the leash is necessary to keep the dog with you, just drop it and let him drag it to make the retrieve.

When you throw the dummy, it will naturally be thrown away from the decoys. The pup is already enthusiastic about fetching dummies, so he may ignore the decoys completely. If he does show interest, step between him and the decoy to discourage him, and say NO.

Don't yell the NO. Don't jump between Duke and the decoy. Don't do anything bombastic that might inhibit Duke during a retrieve. Retrieving should always be fun. Instead, say NO as Mayo Kellogg does it—a quiet NO as in nope. In most cases, that's all it takes.

If your dog is persistent about trying to fetch the decoy, snap the leash on him and walk out to the dummy, but deny him the fun of getting it. Pick it up yourself. Return to the starting point, and try it over. This time, however, spin the dummy, saying "Watch! Watch!" excitedly to get the dog's full attention, and throw it only a few feet away so it's more tempting than the decoys. Repeat this until the pup forgets everything but the dummy.

When you've discouraged Duke from fetching decoys, step just behind the stool before making the throw. Now he must run through the decoys to fetch the dummy. Again, you're close and can stop him if this is too much temptation.

As the dog becomes more and more reliable about avoiding decoys, you can move farther and farther back. At last, it's a dry-land mini-staging of a dog making his fetch through a stool at the duck blind. And you've very nearly gotten something for nothing. All you've really done is give Duke his usual fetch practice. A couple extra moments scattering decoys and saying a few NO's has Speed-Trained Duke into retrieving only what he's sent after. Practice so he doesn't forget.

Start sending the dog for every fetch with a hand signal, and it will gradually teach Duke to take a line.

He learns to leave in the direction the hand points.

Important: At this point, you're sending the pup with FETCH as soon as the dummy is in the air. Be quick with the command because he'll go when he sees the dummy fly, and the command shouldn't come after he's gone. Also, it's important to use your hand to gesture ahead of his nose toward the dummy. It won't mean much now, but repetition will gradually condition the pup to taking direction from you (taking a line, it's called), and learning it this way will save lots of time later.

Step 9

Deciding Who's Top Dog

If you've followed instructions up to this point, you've allowed your dog to advance at his own pace. He might be 12 or 14 weeks old right now, or 4 or 5 months. Age, for the most part, doesn't matter. The important thing has been to move the dog along as rapidly as he has the ability to accept training in order to fully develop his genetic potential. But we haven't crowded the pup. We've been firm with the dog at times, but we've never wilted him with anger. No whippings or beatings have been applied to pressure him into advancing at a rate beyond his natural ability.

Right now you may be saying, "Yeah, all that nice guy stuff, and what has it gotten me? A dog that won't listen, that's what. He needs a good thrashing!"

If these are your thoughts, chances are your pup is about 4 months old. This is one canine behavior that *is* age-linked—not precisely, it does vary with individuals—in all dogs, and it's more pronounced in males. In varying degrees, all dogs go through this business of testing you to see who's boss—and they are all roughly the same age. Expect it again between 11 and 14 months. The worst comes somewhere around 24 months. It's like children going through their "terrible twos" and all the phases that follow, except that dogs don't seem to have as many.

How do you handle this? You can beat the tar out of Duke and prove who's boss. With that, you may regain control but you lose much of the dog's boldness and confidence. You introduce inhibitions that greatly reduce the dog's ability to become a superior hunter. He'll never develop to his full genetic potential, even if later trained by a good professional.

There's a better way. Animal behaviorist Steve Rafe, an extremely perceptive dogman, recommends maintaining or regaining control in the same way that dogs control other dogs. This is natural canine behavior that dogs readily find quite acceptable. Rather than develop distrust and animosities between you and Duke as beatings will do, Rafe's method of control actually bonds the dog closer to you through the natural loyalty canines feel toward their proven superiors.

Although the dog feels compelled to try for control, when he fails he seems quite content to accept the submissive role. In fact, in my experiences, once the contest is over, the dog's happiness seems to be enhanced by knowing his position. Apparently, being sure of his role is comfortable while uncertainty is stressful.

Tight confinement and watching another dog getting to be active are convincing medicine that makes Duke believe training is fun time after all.

If Duke is only being uncooperative during obedience training, controlling him won't take extraordinary measures. Sometimes the young dog is so full of energy at this age that he finds it hard to settle down and concentrate on what you want. If that seems to be the case, take him for his walk first. Practice quartering into the wind and retrieving downwind. Try obedience again after you've worn him down a bit.

On the other hand, Duke might just be disinterested today. When that happens, end the session short. But don't end it on a bad note. What does the dog do best? It's probably something simple from his early training. Have him do it so you're able to stop with praise. Then confine him in a cage or on a two-foot chain for 30 minutes. Don't put him in the kennel. That's not confining enough. Duke probably isn't cooperating because he prefers complete freedom to do whatever he wants. When the reverse happens, and his behavior results in far less freedom a few times, he'll soon realize it's much more fun doing what you want.

In human terms, this is an affectionate gesture. Dogs interpret a paw, leg, or head over the neck as an attempt to exercise control.

If they don't care to accept you as top dog, they'll try to slip out from under your arm.

If you conclude the problem is more than lack of cooperation – Duke is testing your authority – it's time for Rafe's canine-control moves. Go to the dog. Kneel beside him. If you're right-handed, place your left arm over the dog's shoulders.

Dogs place paws or heads over other dog's shoulders or necks to test who is top dog, so Duke may not like it. He may try to slip out from under your arm. Don't allow it. Restrain him by the neck, or collar, or whatever means seem handy at the time.

Disclaimer: Most dogs don't bite their masters, but there are no guarantees. A few dogs bite out of fear. Most bite because they've been allowed to learn they can be dominant, and they intend to defend that status. If this occurred because you're a little afraid of the dog, exercise caution. Dogs can sense fear. And don't try any of these control moves on a strange dog unless you're an experienced trainer. In other words, you are on your own. If you are bitten, we are not responsible.

If the dog declines your control, carry it a step further. Keep the arm over the shoulder, and grip the entire muzzle with your other hand. Bring your face close to leave the impression that it may be your mouth grasping Duke's muzzle.

If Duke continues to show discomfort with the test of your control, carry it one step further. In this situation, the dog doing the testing would grab the other dog's muzzle with his teeth. You can do exactly that. However, if you don't have a "taste" for this sort of work (pardon the pun), you can do a good imitation. Grab Duke's entire muzzle within your right hand (left arm is still over his shoulder) and bring your face right up against his. The hand/face combination isn't that much different from actually gripping the dog with your teeth, but it may be far more safe and sanitary. We both know what places that dog has been licking.

If Duke doesn't care to submit to your control, his eyes will roll. Hang on. He may struggle. Respond with an occasional quick shake of his muzzle. When he settles down, accepting your control, go back to obedience training.

Being picked up and shaken by the scruff of the neck works well, too. If he still tries to defy you, grab his collar for safe control with your right hand (see Disclaimer), and reach under his body to grab legs on the opposite side. It's a struggle sometimes, but yank them out from under him, and flop him on his side. Pick him up to flop him, if necessary. Lie down on Duke, face to face, and hold him there while again you grip his muzzle, giving it short, quick shakes.

Don't expect a turnaround of behavior in one lesson. Repeat it as often as necessary. Duke won't require many at 4 months. In fact, it's highly unlikely that you'll have to go through this whole routine with a 4-month pup. But now you know what to do (and do carefully, because these are critical stages) if defiance becomes stronger at a year and two years. Duke is almost sure to need stronger measures around two. We will cover that in *Part 2, Step 12.*

Step 10

Mid-phase Obedience

With Duke under control again, it's time to go on with obedience training. Maybe Duke is really Duchess, and she didn't even try to defy you. But don't laugh too soon at your male-owning buddies. Some females become so obstinate when they come in season that you just might as well hang it up for three weeks until it's over.

Of course, some females, and males as well, are such agreeable creatures that defiance is scarcely noticeable, regardless of their stage in life or condition. Some of these dogs wilt easily, so if you have one, don't pressure it.

It's often possible to tell how much pressure a dog can take by its behavior under the HEEL command. Tough, bold dogs tend to forge ahead. Soft dogs usually hang back.

Crowding Duke against a fence if he tries to forge ahead of you will speed-train him to HEEL in the right place.

No matter which type you have, dogs seldom care to HEEL in the right place. A hunter can't tolerate a bold dog forging ahead and trying to leave him. Most trainers tap this dog on the nose with a stick or twirl the end of the leash so he'll get clipped if he tries to pull forward. It's much faster, I find, and less abusive, if you HEEL the dog along a fence. Position him between you and the fence and on leash. When he tries to forge as you walk, crowd him against the fence. He'll pull back. If crowded too much, he'll try to come around back to your right. Prevent this with the leash.

HEEL a bold dog counter-clockwise to speed-train his position at your side.

Running into your leg repeatedly teaches Duke to HEEL in the right place. Keep the leash behind your body.

HEEL a soft dog clockwise to speed-train position.

Duke is being urged to keep up in order to HEEL in the right place. Keep the leash in front of your body.

If no fence is available, HEEL the dog in circles. If you have a bold dog, circle counterclockwise. The dog is at your left as you do this, so every time he tries to forge ahead, he tangles with your legs and soon learns to stay in position with his head near your side. If necessary, and it will be at first, shorten the circle whenever needed to make sure Duke gets walked over when he tries to move ahead.

If Duke is soft and hangs back, walk in clockwise circles. This naturally urges him to hurry and catch up because it always appears he's falling behind. Help with an occasional tug and GOOD HEEL! whenever the dog is in correct position.

When you can't HEEL in circles or along a fence, use a leafy limb to keep the dog in position.

When you're in the field and want to practice HEEL while coming back to the kennel or car, you won't be able to go in circles, obviously. Yank off about four feet of thin, green tree limb with plenty of leaves on the end. Swish it across the face of the dog when he tries to forge ahead. I find that the sound effect of the leaves is much more effective than constantly rapping the dog across the nose with a broomstick and much less resented by the dog as well. Even slapping the dog across the muzzle with the leafy end, if necessary, is more sound effect than pain, but it works much better than a stick.

Soft dogs usually need a few well-timed jerks on the leash and lots of GOOD HEEL praise to urge them to keep up. Use the leafy limb if they try to sneak around to your right side.

The training pole adopted from a coonhound training technique teaches a pup to HEEL in exactly the right place at all times.

When some dogs learn you want them to HEEL at your side, they decide that *against* your side is even better. Obedience competitors like that kind of tight HEEL, but you want a loose HEEL for hunting. It's one thing for a dog's head to be glued at your thigh on the clipped grass of an obedience ring. It's quite another when you're trying to sneak up on ducks in a pothole with Duke at HEEL, and he keeps crowding you into the bushes.

I have a simple training pole that I adapted from a coonhound-training method. I use it to make the transitions between SIT at your side and SIT anywhere he is when you order it. See *Part 2, Step 1* for details. It's also useful for establishing the correct distance for the dog at HEEL. With both of your hands on the pole, the dog can't be anywhere else.

The pole also works very well for correcting the forger or lagger. Naturally, you won't carry a pole to the field, but you could use it for early training to establish position, then switch to leash or check cord later.

Don't rely entirely on one method. Know all the ways that speed HEEL training, and use the one appropriate for the dog or the moment. Dogs are more consistent if they learn that you have a variety of ways to enforce your commands, and if they learn in a variety of locations.

Important: If you release Duke directly from HEEL, he'll always be trying to anticipate the command and break early. Instead, always SIT him before the ALL RIGHT release. And SIT him several times during each HEEL session so he doesn't know which SIT will precede the release.

The check cord guarantees compliance to the trilling whistle for COME.

Practice COME while in the field doing quartering lessons or, if the dog won't be hunting upland game, while just going for a walk. Let Duke drag a check cord. Once in a while pick up the cord as he goes by, give the trilling whistle, order COME, and be prepared to gently, but firmly, urge him in with the cord if he doesn't respond immediately. Praise highly, no matter if he came willingly or had to be urged with the cord.

Extra important: Don't make a pest of yourself by calling in the dog too often or every time he gets interested in something. That promotes disobedience. Instead watch for moments when you won't have to distract him from something else, perhaps when he's turning away from something and already looking toward you, or when he's changing direction and already sort of coming your way. Choose the times when obeying COME is easy, then make Duke's obedience fun when he arrives by acting as if he's a dear friend you haven't seen in 10 years.

Super important: Never give just one COME command during your time in the field because it will surely be given when you're ready to go home. Duke will clue in on that about the second time you do it and will thereafter try to avoid going home by not obeying COME.

Turn the left side to the dog as he approaches.

Practice SIT with the COME command. As the dog arrives, turn your left side to him, blow one sharp blast on the whistle, say SIT, and push his rear down if he's slow about doing it. Don't forget the GOOD SIT! because sitting is important for retrievers, yet few enjoy doing it because it stops them, and they'd rather be romping.

Move back a couple of steps, and move from side to side to make Duke understand he must STAY even though you move.

Eventually, circle the dog.

Do the STAY as learned earlier. Simultaneously step forward with the *right* leg, bring the palm of your right hand before his face, and say STAY! The check cord is in your left hand, and you're only one step away, so if he moves, reach out to jerk him back.

Gradually, you'll be able to move from side to side without your motion urging Duke to break command. Then move farther and farther to either side, and eventually circle the dog. When he holds for this, do the same thing two steps away instead of one. Then three, four, and so on until you can walk a considerable distance with Duke at STAY.

Some trainers don't bother with STAY, saying SIT should be adequate because the dog should SIT until released anyhow. I like the extra STAY command because I feel it speeds the dog's understanding of what he should do. It's two different restrictive actions and two different commands. He goes down at SIT when he'd rather be running, and he holds for STAY when he'd rather break. STAY adds emphasis, I believe, that more quickly clues the dog in on the fact that he must stay put until released.

As before, do not yet break the STAY command with COME. Walk away as far as you can at this point, but come back and ATTA BOY him before saying ALL RIGHT and moving on. This promotes a good solid STAY, you will remember, rather than having the dog eagerly waiting to break.

One more tip: Never beg or plead with a dog. Order him. But do it in a firm voice – *NOT* a scream or roar. And never give an order you can't enforce. If you encounter an impossible situation – perhaps the partially trained pup decides to chase the neighbor's cat – just keep your mouth shut. In this situation, yelling COME only teaches Duke that it's possible to ignore your commands. Let it happen. Then, later, go back and set up the same situation, but control Duke with a check cord, and give him a rude awakening.

Step 11

Mid-phase Land Retrieving

You can do the mid-phase obedience, land retrieving, and nose training (*Part 1, Step 12*) all in the same session. It needn't be lengthy. About 20 minutes every other day will do it. Because the activities are so varied, the dog can take more, if you like, but an average of 10 minutes a day can Speed-Train him into a good hunting retriever.

Spin the dummy in a clockwise motion.

Retrieving now becomes a little more structured than it was during play-fetch, but we'll make the changes gradually. SIT-STAY Duke at your left side. Maybe you've just been throwing the dummy underhanded during play-fetch. We need a little more distance now, so tie a foot of cord to the dummy's eyelet. Spin the dummy by the cord in a clockwise motion. When you let go, the centrifugal force will carry the dummy considerably farther than you can throw it, and because it's spinning clockwise, you'll let go during the lower portion of its arc which means it will leave at a dog's eye level. As you spin, say WATCH to get Duke's attention, and let fly. Getting his attention and releasing the dummy at eye level are both important in teaching the pup to begin marking falls, or in other words, remembering where the dummy (and later the bird) hit the ground.

Time for the COME command — just as the pup reaches for the dummy.

Tweet-tweet the whistle, say FETCH, and let Duke go with the dummy. Don't restrain him before he's sent at this point. It could have inhibiting results. Watch carefully as he runs, and just as he reaches for the dummy, right before he has it, shout COME! This programs his brain to run back to you the instant he grabs the dummy instead of perhaps suddenly deciding that this time maybe he'll go off somewhere and keep the prize for himself. Because Duke probably knows the verbal COME better than the long trill on the whistle, and because timing is so important, in this instance we won't blow the whistle first. You can blow it for reinforcement after the verbal command, of course. Doing so helps develop Duke's response to whistle commands, an essential in the really finished hunting retriever.

Turning away reinforces delivery. Do it squatting now, standing later.

Turn your left side to accept the dummy from Duke. Remember that he's coming alongside when you're turning away as if to leave. Your motion urges him to follow, brings him in closer, and tends to prevent the habit of dropping the dummy in front of you from ever starting. That habit becomes very serious business the first time a cripple flies off as a result of Duke dropping it out of your reach.

Don't let him drop the dummy, and help him respond to SIT.

Just as Duke pulls alongside, reach under his chin to prevent him from dropping the dummy. Simultaneously, blow a sharp blast for SIT, followed by dropping the whistle from your mouth and giving the verbal command. If he doesn't sit quickly enough, raise his head with the right hand you have under his chin, and push his rump down with your left. Let him hold the dummy for a few seconds, then say GIVE and take your hand from under his chin to accept the dummy.

Most trainers that have a dummy-dropping dog will step back, or even run backward, under the theory that the dog will hurry to catch up, won't drop the dummy while moving, and the trainer can take the dummy when the dog does catch up. Our Speed-Training method of turning our left side to the dog will prevent most of this. If our dog is a real problem dropper, we, too, can take a step or two away or even run. Because we're also already facing in the same direction as the dog, we'll find it easier to move because we won't be going clumsily backward.

Another stunt to prevent dropping is to flutter a handkerchief in your hand as the dog approaches with the dummy. It gets the dog's attention and causes him to raise his head to look up instead of running head low and dropping the dummy. Or throw from beside a tree, car, building, or whatever, then duck behind and make the dog look for you. He comes upon you suddenly, and you have the dummy before he can drop it.

He won't give up the dummy? Give him more than he wants.

He'll probably eject it forcefully.

Many dogs are happy to push the dummy out with their tongues. Some, however, would rather not give it up. Don't fight it. Don't EVER play tug of war for the dummy and start a hardmouth habit. If he wants to hang on, just push the dummy farther back into his mouth. It will begin to gag him, and he'll push it out.

Mayo Kellogg wiggles his fingers to beckon a pup around to the left side.

The pup is attracted by the motion and follows.

Mayo switches the wiggling to his left hand fingers, and the pup goes all the way around.

And now praise for the correct delivery.

If you have a dog that would rather keep the dummy, dropping it at your feet isn't likely to become a problem. You may want to train this dog's delivery a little differently. Some hunters like a retriever to come in on the right, go around the back, come to the left, and sit before giving up the dummy or bird. Mayo Kellogg has a clever trick for accomplishing this. He starts it while the pup is very young — at the time when Mayo is still squatting to urge the pup to come in. Mayo's right hand is extended, and just as the pup arrives, Mayo wiggles his fingers. The pup is attracted by the motion, so Mayo brings his wiggling fingers around to the back. The pup follows them. When Mayo's right hand is as far as it will go, the fingers of his left hand take over the wiggling to lure the pup the rest of the way around. The pup is then seated and the dummy taken.

Don't forget the most important part of every good retrieve the dog makes: ATTA BOY! But make a rule: He earns the ATTA BOY; no delivery to hand, no ATTA BOY. Never be tempted to praise before the retrieve is completed. The dog may decide the important part is done when you give the premature praise and become sloppy about finishing. Call a halt after just a few retrieves. More fetches are not necessary to teach the dog, and it's important to stop while the pup is still excited over what he's doing.

Important: Dropping or fumbling the dummy may be quite normal if your pup is only 3½ to 4½ months old. Before worrying about a cure, check to see if the pup is teething and has a tender mouth. If so, temporarily retire the canvas dummies, and go back to a softsock dummy, or use a rubber ball or glove.

Equally important: Never use just one dummy. Duke will get the notion that this one thing is all he's supposed to fetch. And yes, he can tell the difference between dummies by their odors.

Extra important: At this point in training, always have the wind at your back as you throw the dummy. Send Duke downwind to fetch. Dogs always run straighter lines going downwind. In the interest of Speed-Training, we want our dog to make a habit of taking straight lines. If you send him across wind, he'll veer off with the wind. Whatever way he starts will tend to become a habit.

Super important: Never step forward to accept a dummy. The dog will probably stop and drop the dummy. A terrible habit is started. If you turn your left side to the dog as we recommend, you won't be tempted into making this mistake.

Step 12

Nose Training

Maybe Duke is already quartering well. Maybe you're having a whole lot of trouble getting him away from your side. Either way, he'll benefit from nose training. If he's quartering, he'll have to hunt cover, not run around it. If he's not leaving your side, the enticing smell will draw him out.

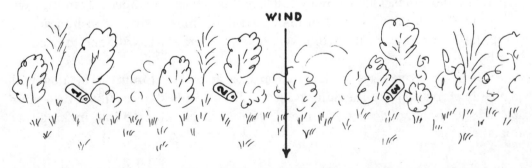

Properly planted scented dummies teach Duke to use his nose.

Dunk four Bob West feather dummies, or homemade feather dummies, or liberally scented canvas dummies in a bucket of water. Find a place where tall cover edges a short-cropped, easy place to run. It might be where the lawn borders woods in a park, or a grown-over fencerow along a field or pasture. Check the wind. Choose a place where the wind is blowing over the tall cover and toward the short-cropped place. If the dog runs the edge of high cover, he'll have to get a whiff and become interested.

Go out by yourself to plant the dummies. Twirl one and see how far it will fly. Judge the distance and try to stay that far away when you throw three of the four dummies in different places just inside the tall cover. We don't want Duke to learn he can track our own scent trail to the dummies.

Walk back and get Duke and the fourth wet dummy. Have him make a couple of simple retrieves with this dummy as you enter the field. Now he has this interesting scent on his mind. Put the fourth dummy back in your training vest or coat, and snap the check cord onto Duke's collar.

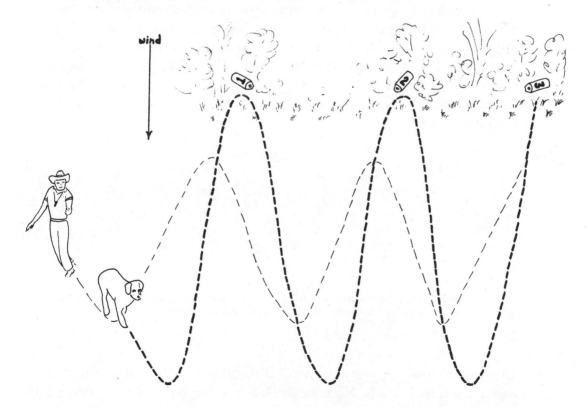

By finding dummies inside the edge of heavy cover, the dog learns where to search for game.

If the dog won't leave your side, just walk along the cover's edge until he smells the first dummy and can't resist charging into the weeds to get it. Say FETCH if he hesitates. Praise him highly when he delivers the dummy.

If he's quartering, let him swing back and forth while traveling parallel to the high cover edge. Every time he makes the swing on one side, he'll be at that high cover edge. See to it that one of the swings takes him right where the wind will blow scent from the dummy to him. When he catches the scent and shows interest, give him slack—let go of the check cord, if necessary—so he has no trouble getting to the dummy. Again, say FETCH if he hesitates. Say COME just as he's grabbing for it, and ATTA BOY him something fierce when he makes the delivery.

Repeat this with the second and third planted dummies. After that, do a few mid-phase land retrieves, practice mid-phase obedience, and call it a day. Give him the next day off to meditate on the miracle of bird scent and to wonder if he'll ever smell it again.

On the second day, go back to exactly the same spot. (If the wind is wrong, wait until a day when it's right.) Even many days later, a decently intelligent dog will remember where he found the scented dummies. If he hasn't wanted to leave your side, I wager he will when he nears the old locations. Make sure the dummies are thrown in almost exactly the same place they were the first time. If he's quartering well, do the same procedure, anyway. It's teaching Duke to hunt cover.

Discontinue number 1 dummy and add number 4 to teach your dog to keep searching— there always may be another dummy (bird) to be found out there.

After another session or two, give Duke a surprise. Discontinue planting Number 1 dummy. But add Number 4. He'll be disappointed that there's no dummy where he thought there should be one, but he's learning that likely cover isn't always productive. Go on and search elsewhere. He'll expect numbers 2 and 3 and be quite happy. But again, on you go to the surprise finding of Number 4. He's learning something new. Check likely places, but don't quit. There's probably another dummy (bird) to be found out there somewhere.

The next time you train, quit Number 2 and add Number 5, and so on thereafter – always dropping one of the familiar places and adding a new one.

Gradually move the scented dummies farther into cover so he becomes more interested in searching the heavy stuff.

Try to find a place where tall cover, perhaps bushes or clumps of taller weeds, stands out as different and might be recognized as objectives – places the pup should check for birds. Plant dummies and quarter Duke into them from the downwind side.

Important: Scenting is difficult for dogs on dry, hot, and windy days. Try to nose train on cool, overcast, and moist days.

Bonus: You have just Speed-Trained your retriever into the first step of going for blind retrieves. He'll be prepared when you're ready for it in *Step 17.*

Step 13

Mid-phase Water Retrieves

We've introduced Duke to water. Presumably, it's warm, and he enjoys it, so let's get him started right. Get the shotgun. Work the action on the way to the kennel. Duke sees you coming with a brisk step and knows something is about to happen that involves him. Otherwise, you wouldn't be walking toward him. And you don't walk that briskly when coming out to mow the lawn or gawk at the gladiolus. Duke clues in quickly on body language. Besides that, we've taught Duke that the shotgun signals something good about to happen. Right now, the thing he wants most is for that gate to open. The shotgun is in your hand. Open the gate, and just as Duke comes racing through, work the action.

If you're driving to water, SIT Duke at the vehicle. Order GET IN, and work the shotgun action just as he jumps.

When you get to the lake, pond, or whatever, give Duke three or four very simple retrieves, and work the shotgun action as the dummy is in the air. Duke is probably in the air himself by that time.

Remember, we have to start Duke right. If we're going to Speed-Train, we can't make mistakes because bad habits take more time to correct than good habits take to learn. So, that means be careful how you accept these three or four simple retrieves. In fact, be careful how you accept water retrieves from this moment on.

Avoid dummy dropping by meeting Duke at the water's edge.

Position yourself at the water's edge so you can accept the dummy immediately. Turn your left side to him as usual so he'll feel the natural urge to catch up. But SIT him, and say GIVE the instant he's out of water.

There's very good reason for this caution. Water retrieves are different than land retrieves. The dog is soaking wet, so his first impulse on leaving the water is to shake himself. A great many dogs do not feel it's handy to shake with a dummy in the mouth, so they drop it first. Some pick it up again to finish the retrieve. Others assume the retrieve is finished. It's only a matter of time until *any* dog that drops will drop a cripple that escapes.

So once again we'll have to put an *important* in the middle of the text for emphasis. *Under no circumstances may you fail to praise the dog when the dummy is delivered to hand during a water retrieve.* By the same token, *never* praise the dog if he drops the dummy. I hope you see the importance of *never* praising *before* a retrieve is completed to hand whether it's on land or water. Being consistent with the praise at the right moment, and none at all for failing to deliver, is essential in Speed-Training a dog not to drop.

As Duke acquires experience in water retrieves, you very gradually move back from the shoreline to accept the dummy. Always turn the left side to him so you're prepared to take a quick step or two away if he shows signs of wanting to drop the dummy. Say COME as you do so to add encouragement. If a mistake is made, *don't* become angry. Just don't praise him. And start accepting the retrieves closer to shore again. You can't permit yourself the slightest anger during retrieves. You can't inhibit or frighten away the dog you want to come to you with something he'd just as soon keep himself anyway.

Some dogs, in fact, may decide they won't come out of the water where you're standing. They'll just swim out somewhere else and keep the dummy for themselves this time. This occurs mostly during those 4-, 11-to-14, and 24-month defiant stages. Don't stand there and stew. And don't yell and scream. Just walk along the shoreline and take the dummy no matter where the blockhead comes out. He'll soon learn it doesn't work.

Working close at first, and using a splash pole, assures that the dog doesn't fetch decoys.

When Duke is doing well on simple, short retrieves, and delivering to hand without problems, you'll want to work with decoys. Place the decoys close enough so you can reach Duke with your 10-foot pole. Throw the dummy among the decoys and send the dog. If he starts making the switch to a decoy, get the pole between him and the decoy, and quietly say NO. Slap the surface making a splash or repeated splashes, if necessary, to distract the dog. Rarely is it necessary to tap the dog.

As Duke improves in his water retrieves, don't discontinue praising him. Whenever possible, also continue to involve the noise of the shotgun action.

Sloppy water entry can be cured by keeping the dog on hold (SIT-STAY) until the suspense is killing him.

If your dog starts to lose interest, you may be overdoing it. It may be necessary to reduce the number of retrieves. A better way to stimulate interest is to not let the dog go after every retrieve. It makes him more consistent about going reliably when sent if you'll occasionally just keep him on SIT-STAY and fetch the dummy yourself. You did that on land. Now wade out, or row your boat out, to fetch the dummy yourself about once every five or six times.

If the dog is just tiptoeing into the water instead of hitting it with an enthusiastic splash (he wants to retrieve, but his entry is sloppy), the cure is much the same, but you won't need a dummy. Wade or row out, and hold Duke on SIT-STAY until the suspense is killing him. When you say COME, he'll hit the water eagerly. Repeat until enthusiastic entry becomes a habit.

You will remember that our rule during obedience has been to never break STAY with COME. This will not be a permanent rule, but it is very important in early Speed-Training. Breaking the rule now for the first time provides even more motivation for Duke to charge into the water. For now, however, do not break STAY with COME for any reason except to correct sloppy entry.

The next thing Duke needs to learn is that there are times when a duck or other bird may fall on land beyond the water. This may sound simple to you, but it isn't to him. So far, you've thrown a dummy on land, and he has found it on land. When he has been sent into water, he has found it on water. If he goes across to the opposite shore, and still hasn't found the dummy, he's confused.

Teach Duke now to cross water to fetch on land, and later, more complicated falls across water will come easier.

To Speed-Train Duke into crossing water to retrieve from land, look for a small ditch. Maybe there's a finger off your pond or lake. It's ideal if it's very narrow at the far end and fairly wide where it joins the main body of water. Or maybe you can find a creek with wide and narrow spots.

Anyhow, begin by throwing the dummy across a narrow ditch where Duke can easily see it and only has to splash through a little water to get it. Gradually work across wider and wider water, always throwing the dummy just onto the opposite bank. Later we'll teach him that birds don't always fall on the bank, either, but he's not quite ready for that.

Important: Never think because a dog does something once that he has learned it. Dogs are habitual. Nothing is ever learned until he has done it often enough to be a habit. It usually takes a dog about as long for something to become a habit as it does for him to learn it. *If* it takes Duke two weeks to really learn a move like fetching across water, be sure to practice it for at least another two weeks. After that, occasional refreshers are enough.

Step 14

Doubles, Triples, and Marking

Have you heard of ground cable tie-outs? Not many dogmen have. But I plan to change that; the ground cable is the handiest gadget for retriever training that I've seen since someone adopted canvas-covered boat bumpers for use as dummies. The minute Tom Scott told me he intended to make and market a ground cable tie-out, and described how it's used, ideas started flashing in my mind on how it could solve retriever training problems. We experimented, it worked, and before Tom even got into production he had decided to offer a model in custom lengths to be used as a trainer.

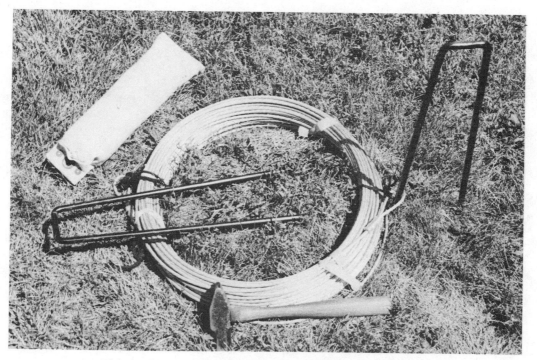

This is the simple, but amazingly useful, training cable.

The ground cable tie-out is simple. It's a quality, heavy-duty, several-stranded cable held stretched out on the ground by stakes at each end. A short cable has a ring on one end which allows it to slide up and down the main cable. The other end of the short cable has a bolt snap which attaches to the dog's collar, of course. The dog now has full run of the cable which can be as long as you have room for. It's much better than a chain. It can even turn corners and surround your property—or make a dog turn in a desired direction during training. (We'll show you how that's done later.)

Our first, although not most important, use for the training cable will be starting Duke on doubles and triples. Getting the dog to go after the dummy he is sent for instead of the last one he saw thrown is half the training problem. Later, there may be real need to send him for the first duck shot instead of the last, which he remembers best, because the first one is disappearing down the river. The other half of the training problem is getting Duke to use his head to mark falls; for example, to remember well enough where each bird fell that he can fetch one after the other.

Let Duke go with the second dummy.

The training problem vanishes with use of the cable. SIT-STAY Duke on your left somewhere near the cable's mid-point. Attach him to the short cable, and stand in the way or hold onto the short cable so he can't go when you throw the first dummy near the cable a short distance to your right. Toss a second dummy to your left, and say FETCH as you do so. Let him go with this throw.

Without the cable, he could switch and go for the first dummy. On the cable, he can't. You're in the way, so we'll make him mark (remember) the first dummy thrown.

Send Duke after the first dummy thrown by giving him plenty of hand and body motion.

When Duke arrives with the first dummy, SIT him. Praise him. Then with hand and body motion, plus *tweet-tweet* on the whistle and a verbal FETCH, send him after the other dummy.

If he doesn't remember that first dummy thrown, toss a rock or dirt clod in its direction so he sees it and goes.

When Duke becomes good at this sequence, switch it so you're sending him after the first dummy first and the second dummy last. This is more taxing on his memory, but as we said earlier, it may become very essential.

Toss numbers 1 and 2, then walk out to plant number 3. Send him for number 2 first to make him exercise his memory.

Practice until Duke is reliable at doing doubles both ways. Then plant a third dummy about two feet farther down the cable than where Number 1 will fall. Just walk it down the cable. It won't hurt if Duke sees where you put it. We're developing his memory, anyway. Throw the dummies. Send him for Number 1. He'll see Number 3 a couple feet ahead as he grabs Number 1 and have his memory refreshed. But don't send him for it yet. First, we send him in the opposite direction down the cable to Number 2. Finally, he goes for Number 3.

Practice by placing Number 3 farther and farther down the cable before throwing 1 and 2 to their usual positions. Eventually, he can't see Number 3 when picking up Number 1, but if you do it gradually enough, he'll know it's there from past experience and go anyway. It helps considerably if the cable is laid so he's running into the wind to get this Number 3 dummy. Obviously, it also helps to use a scented or feather dummy.

After a pattern is established, switch directions and start over so the dog isn't always going down the same end of the cable for the two dummies.

Bonus 1: While introducing your dog to doubles and triples, you've already Speed-Trained him into an introduction to becoming steady. Being steady is not going for a retrieve until sent. Until now, he usually went when he saw the dummy fly. We restrained him from going during this step in training, which we'll build on to make him steady in *Step 16.*

Bonus 2: Think about the Number 3 dummy which you always carried out instead of throwing. He never, ever saw it fall, yet he went after it. We've Speed-Trained him into making blind retrieves which we'll also build on later. If we start this early, we have him raring to go—always excitedly thinking maybe there's one more dummy out there to fetch and get praised for.

Reminder: We can't keep saying PRAISE THE DOG after each new training step we introduce, but by now I'm sure you know that. Also, use the shotgun as a signal of fun to come, and work the action before many of the retrieves. And keep using both whistle and verbal commands.

Important: We're beginning to get into more advanced training, but that doesn't mean we can slack up on basics. COME, SIT, STAY, DOWN, GET IN, HEEL, simple fetches, and turning to the whistle during quartering should be run through frequently but quickly. It keeps Duke sharp and gives him great confidence when he can go through these simple routines with ease. He's a bolder hunter that finds it easier to learn each new thing.

Step 15

*Doubles, Triples in Decoys—
Land and Water*

As soon as Duke is handling tossed doubles, plus the planted triple, on the cable, and doing it without attempting to switch to a decoy instead of the dummy sent for, he can advance to doubles in decoys.

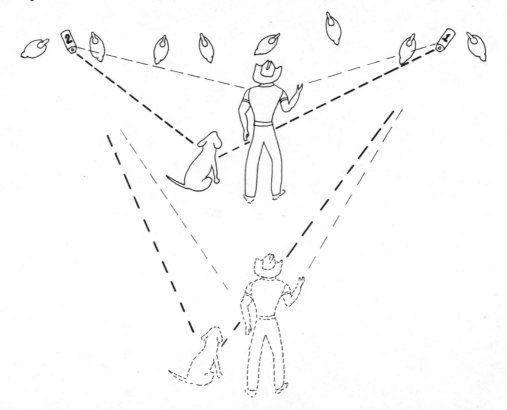

Stand close to minimize the temptation to switch dummies. As Duke becomes reliable about fetching the dummy sent for, you can back off to narrow the angle between the dummies.

Spread the decoys rather thinly over an area of grass about 50 feet wide. Stand with the dog very close to the spread, and toss a dummy to each far edge. Restrain Duke from going for the first throw. Use a check cord for control. Once again, we're developing Duke's marking memory and establishing discipline so we can direct our dog to whatever fall we want fetched first.

The dog has been introduced to decoys already, but they will be an added temptation and distraction nevertheless. Send him after the Number 1 throw. If he tries to switch to Number 2, stop him with the check cord and start over. No anger. He'll get it. But if he doesn't do it right, he doesn't get to fetch. Place him at SIT-STAY. Fetch the dummies yourself. This time, don't throw them as far into the decoys.

You'll notice on the diagram that we've started the dog from a position right up against the decoys. Why didn't we move back? Remember the reason for the cable? Duke could only go right or left. Once started toward a dummy, he'd be unlikely to reverse himself and try to switch to the other. For that same reason, we toss the dummies to widely separated positions in the decoys. At this point, if the two dummies were just a few feet apart, Duke wouldn't know which one he was sent for and would have difficulty making up his mind.

If your dog tries to fetch a decoy, give him a jerk on the check cord and a quiet NO. Bring him back with COME and the cord. Fetch it yourself with him on SIT-STAY. Not getting to fetch the dummy when he tries to switch, tries to grab a decoy, or forgets to mark the falls will make him pay more attention next time.

As Duke becomes good at widely separated dummies in decoys, you can move back from the spread to send him and you can narrow the width of the spread. All this narrows the angle between the throws and introduces greater temptation to switch. Again, stop him and complete the retrieve yourself whenever he goes for the wrong dummy. But go slow on narrowing this angle so you don't confuse him.

We've made Duke wait before going for the Number 1 dummy until Number 2 is thrown in order to teach marking memory. But this isn't always the retrieving sequence while hunting. We also need control, so when Duke is going well on the 1-2 pattern, switch to 2-1. When he understands both ways while going through decoys, switch frequently so he has to remember the falls and also let you decide which he'll fetch first.

With a check cord for control against going for the wrong dummy, or fetching dummies, send Duke for doubles in the order you decide.

First to one side . . .

. . . then the other.

Duke is learning to mark, fetch doubles in water, and leave the decoys alone in the process.

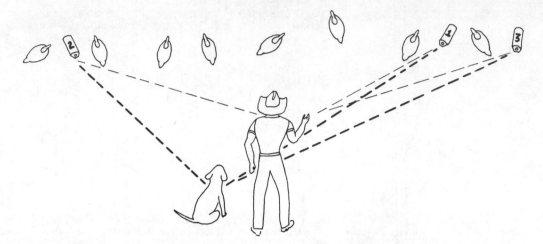

Go back to working close to introduce triples in decoys.

When Duke is reasonably reliable on doubles through decoys (he's too young to be perfect), go back to working close to the spread, and introduce a third dummy on the far edge of the decoys. Send him first for Number 3, the last thrown, so he'll remember it most easily. In addition, he's accustomed to the dummies on the right and left, so he'll know where to go for them. Do 3, 1, 2 sequences and 3, 2, 1 sequences. When he's good on these, switch to 1, 3, 2 and 2, 3, 1 sequences. Finally, do 1, 2, 3 and 2, 1, 3 sequences. When he is successful with all, mix them up any way you want during practice sessions.

If Duke is progressing rapidly and is very young, he may not yet be ready for triples. Don't push him too hard. Wait a few days, and try again. One day he'll put it together.

Repeat this with dummies in the water. With triples, as with doubles, when Duke is doing well, move back from the spread on land to narrow the angles between the throws. In water, move the spread farther out.

Step 16

Lining and Blinds on Cable

Doing doubles and triples on the cable has already Speed-Trained the dog to steadying, taking a straight line, and going for blind retrieves. Now it's time to build on what Duke already knows.

Being steady (not going for a retrieve before sent) is very important. Some hunters don't mind if their dogs go with the first shot. They even claim they'd rather have the dog on his way so there's less chance of losing the bird. This coin, however, has a stronger flip side. If you missed that first bird, your dog may continue to chase through other birds, flushing them out of range. Maybe you say you'd rather chance losing shots than chance losing a downed or crippled bird. Your friends will disagree violently when Duke is 100 yards away chasing pheasants out the other end of the cover. I think you'll change your mind, too, when you realize that while Duke is chasing, or even retrieving, the first bird, he failed to mark the two that fell later. Had he waited, he could have marked, and retrieved, all three.

Steadying can be very inhibiting to some retrievers, so analyze your dog first. If he tried to forge ahead during HEEL training, and if he breezed through gunfire introduction, he's probably bold enough to deal with steadying easily. If not, exercise caution.

This is the right way to place a choke chain on a dog's neck.

This is wrong. Slide the choke chain off the dog's head, turn it around, and slide it on again.

Place the choke chain on Duke's neck properly. If you place it backward, it will continue to hold and choke after the initial jerk on the chain. If it's placed properly, it tightens and grips the neck uncomfortably, but releases the instant the jerk ends. The idea of the choke chain is to be able to do a quick correction. *You don't pull slowly and hang on. You jerk and release.* In this instance the dog will run before sent and apply his own jerk. But the chain must release when he stops.

Hitting the end of a leash is a good cure for going before sent.

Duke knows that his discomfort was caused by his own action and quickly learns to correct it.

Attach your leash or check cord to the choke chain. This part doesn't have to be done on the cable. Place Duke at SIT-STAY, get a good grip on the leash or cord (wear gloves to avoid rope burns) and throw the dummy. If he breaks the SIT-STAY command and goes before you say FETCH, hang on and let him hit the end of the leash or several feet of check cord.

Make him SIT-STAY while you fetch the dummy.

Bring Duke back and put him on SIT-STAY while you fetch the dummy. Try another throw. If he goes again, he hits the end again. If he goes a third time, don't just hang on. Jerk back hard when he hits the end.

Occasional false throws teach him he doesn't get sent for every dummy.

Also work in a false throw now and then, even after he stops going before being sent. Seeing your arm spring forward may urge him into a false start, too. Raise hell. This helps Speed-Train him into realizing he won't always be sent.

From now on, begin to delay now and then before sending him, so he isn't always hair-triggered to dash for the dummy at your slightest move. Occasionally, walk out and fetch the dummy yourself. It will make him realize he doesn't get every fetch. And get Duke very steady prior to shooting before retrieves. Once the shotgun becomes a part of the retrieve, especially with birds, steadying is very difficult to teach and enforce.

A soft dog is easy to restrain by the collar.

If your dog is soft, use more gentle restraint to avoid inhibiting him. Put him on SIT-STAY, and hold his collar as you throw. Say "No" matter-of-factly, and hang on until he settles down. Then send him with a whistle or vocal FETCH. Repeat until the dog learns to wait. If he doesn't learn in several tries, let him hit the end of the leash. Maybe he wasn't as soft as you thought.

From now on, if you aren't already, always send Duke with the hand signal.

Once the dog realizes he must wait until sent, and is reliable about it, discontinue using the choke chain. Fasten him to the cable by his collar. Your left hand is no longer needed for control, so from now on always use it to send Duke on a line. Position your hand beside the dog's face, and shoot it forward toward the tossed dummy as you say FETCH or *tweet–tweet* the whistle. Lunging a step forward as your hand shoots out will add body language emphasis that helps speed a young dog on his way. Later, with experience, a flick of the hand will suffice.

Important: We should always be reviewing basics. Never assume that because the dog learned them, they cannot be forgotten, or the dog *will* forget them. It's especially important, however, to go through basics before and after working with something as inhibiting as steadying. Going through those old familiar moves, and being praised for doing them right, will restore his confidence.

Equally important: If your dog is very bold, and did not want to become staunch, do all future off-cable training with him dragging the check cord. Not only will it be available for control, he will know that it is. Later, regardless what we're doing, he knows he's controlled when the cord is snapped to his collar. As he accepts control, we can gradually shorten the cord until we're only snapping on a 3-foot rope to drag. But he doesn't look back and measure it. He believes he's controlled. This could be very important during advanced training.

A retriever must learn to take a straight line so he can be sent to a blind fall. It's also the first step in handling with hand signals in advanced training. We've learned that he takes the straightest line downwind, so we've done our fetch practice downwind in an effort to establish that habit. Unfortunately, most retrievers need more than this to keep them from veering off the line.

Trainers have cooked up ingenious ways to keep Duke straight. One is to run him along a fence, which is 100 percent effective if the dog habitually veers in only one direction.

Probably the best lining method has been a long path cut in high weeds. The dog takes the easiest route, which happens to be straight. Other paths were added until the trainer had a baseball diamond cut through the weeds, plus crossing paths that go from home plate to second base, and from third to first. The method is very handy to teach straight lines, and equally useful to teach hand signals during advanced training.

How many of us, though, have backyards that big? And if we do, will *any* of our wives be content with a backyard of grown-up weeds? In fact, will community ordinances allow it?

That's what made the lights go on in my head when I heard about Tom Scott's ground cable tie-out. Here was a simple device that could be used to teach lining. The dog couldn't go anywhere but straight. A short cable could be used on some lawns. Or a long one could be used in a park or someone's pasture. The 100-footer Tom originally sent me wasn't long enough. The 200-footer I now have is far superior.

Both straight lines and blind retrieves are learned at the same time. To get started, drop several dummies at the far end of the cable. Let Duke see you do it. Move him back down the cable a short distance, maybe 20 feet from the dummies. SIT-STAY him, and then give Duke a line with the hand signal and whistle or voice command. He hasn't seen a fall, but he saw you drop the dummies, and he can still see them, so he'll go.

Move back 10 more feet, and send him again. Keep moving back with each retrieve. He knows where the dummies are, so he goes.

When you run out of dummies, HEEL Duke and walk him back to see you drop some more. Walk back to where you last sent him, and send him again. Move back 10 more feet with each group of dummies.

If the grass or weeds are a little high, or the ground is uneven, he may not be able to see the dummies any longer. But he goes anyhow because he knows where they are.

With lots and lots of practice, Duke will eventually go without seeing you drop the dummies. He'll trust that the dummies will be where they always were before.

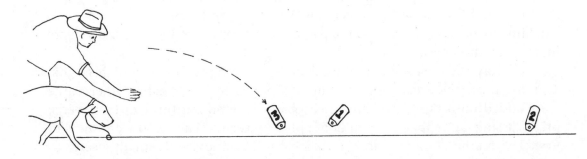

Plant 1 and 2; toss 3, which the dog goes for first. By gradually increasing the distance, Duke will learn to go on faith to fetch dummies that are out of sight.

Now reverse things. Place two dummies beside the cable about 15 and 30 feet away. With Duke on SIT-STAY, throw another dummy two or three feet from the first one you planted. Send him. While fetching it, he'll see the one at 15 feet and remember it's there. When sent for it, he'll see and remember the one at 30 feet.

Gradually work the dummies farther and farther out until Duke is going on faith alone, never seeing a dummy before going. Now he's taking lines for blind retrieves, and practicing straight lines to boot.

Don't overdo any single session. And mix up the methods once Duke learns both ways of going for blinds on a cable.

Important: Never work a dog, especially a pup, on two things in a row that he doesn't like. Keep in mind that dogs have "off days," too. Don't lose your temper. Just work until you can end the session with praise for obeying a simple command, then quit.

Step 17

Gunfire Conditioning

You've already introduced the sight of the shotgun as well as the sound of its action, so Duke has no reason to fear firearms. It's customary to pop blanks in a pistol next, then advance to light loads in a louder .410 or 20 gauge, then heavier loads, then light and heavy in 16 or 12 gauge. In the first place, however, you may not have all of these guns. In the second place, pistols (or rifles) do not sound like shotguns. Forget all that, and use the shotgun your dog will hear on the hunt.

Enlist a friend who likes to shoot. Hand him your shotgun and a box of shells. Have him walk off about 150 yards to a place where he can still be in sight of you.

The best time for Duke to hear gunfire is while he's enjoying himself thoroughly. That way he'll associate gunfire with fun right from the beginning. He loves to retrieve, of course, so that's what he'll be doing while your buddy shoots.

The sequence is: you throw, helper behind you fires, you order FETCH.

Set it up so your friend can see you toss the dummy. He fires when you throw. The sequence is: 1. you throw; 2. he fires; and 3. you order FETCH. Do it smoothly and quickly – no hesitations.

As soon as your gunner fires, he will walk 50 feet closer. That's about 17 steps. He signals with a raised arm when he's ready to shoot again. You throw, he fires, and you order FETCH.

Continue this until the gunner is 75 yards away. Watch Duke during every shot to make sure the noise isn't bothering him. At that distance, it shouldn't. Stop for the day.

Two days later, start the gunner at 100 yards and have him advance 50 feet with every shot until he is within 50 yards. Stop for the day.

Two days later, start at 75 yards. If Duke shows no sign of fear or nervousness, let the gunner advance 50 feet with every shot until he's right beside you. End it by having the gunner fire from the dog's left-rear, left-front, right-front, and right-rear. This should condition him to gunfire from all directions.

If somewhere along the line your dog does exhibit nervousness, stop right there for the day. The next day, go back to the distance where he wasn't nervous and have the gunner advance only 25 feet and shoot two sequences at each location.

When Duke has accepted your friend's presence with the gun, take it yourself and shoot before ordering FETCH.

If your dog accepts gunfire easily, he'll soon decide that this sound is just another part of the order to retrieve. He'll probably start taking off for the dummy the instant he hears the shotgun. Don't worry about it. He anticipated commands before. That's how we taught him whistle commands. Furthermore, some hunters like their dogs to get moving when they hear the gun. If you prefer your dog steady to shot, however, we'll take care of that later. Right now, we're just delighted that the dog isn't gun-shy.

Important: Do not attempt to precede all this by firing over Duke "just once to test him." Yes, if he has no tendencies toward noise shyness, you could eliminate all this time and effort spent conditioning. But one close-up shot – an unexpected, unprecedented surprise, and perhaps shock to the dog – could make him severely gun-shy. After all the time and effort spent training up to this point, nobody in his right mind would risk losing it all.

The gun-shy cure tape is the easiest, most effective, and quickest cure I've found.

If somehow you make your dog gun-shy, it's essential to figure out what you did wrong and change your behavior, but don't take all the blame. I believe many gun-shy dogs have the noise sensitive tendencies in their genes. The breeder should have been more careful. Lots of people disagree with me on this, but invariably they are the ones who got most of their knowledge of heredity right from a book (or from a teacher who got his knowledge from the same book) written by a college professor who never raised anything but his hand when he was in school. If you want to know about heredity, talk to a farmer who earns his living breeding and raising animals. A perceptive husbandman can tell you some amazing things that are inherited. I know of a beagle bitch that balanced on her front legs and raised her rear off the ground to urinate. She threw a female pup that did exactly the same thing from the first time it urinated outside the dog house.

Anyhow, there's hope if you have a gun-shy dog, regardless how it happened. It's a matter of reconditioning this dog's responses, and Steve Rafe has done it with a tape recording. (Write to Rafe at Starfire Enterprises, PO Box 4509, 32 Old Smalleytown Rd., Warren, NJ 07060 for current prices.)

I received one of the pilot tapes and had the satisfying experience of being the first person in the world to cure a gun-shy dog with nothing but a tape recording. Like everyone who does dog training, I've cured gun-shyness with inconsistent success. Knowing how difficult and sometimes impossible it can be, I was amazed by how quick and easy it was with the tape.

The tape starts with nothing but soothing music. You play that several days in a row at feeding time. The next segment has barely audible sounds of shotgun mixed in. Gradually, with each new segment, the sounds of the shotgun become louder until they are as loud as the music. After that, the shotgun blasts remain at maximum while the music diminishes with each segment. Finally, the last segment is nothing but shotgun blasts. At that point, the dog has come to believe that the blasts are as soothing as the music was in the first segment. The tape worked for me exactly as claimed.

I told Steve the tape is even more useful as a gunfire conditioner. You play it at feeding time while displaying the gun, and the dog becomes accustomed to shotgun blasts before you ever fire the first shot.

Important: After a gun-shy dog has become accustomed to the shotgun on tape, I would still play it safe and go through the gunfire conditioning with the friend firing and you throwing dummies. I would repeat it several times, just to be sure, and *I would do it in the same place each time until a pattern is established.* Don't throw a sensitive dog a curve by a surprise shot coming from a new direction. You can condition him to gunfire from new directions after you can fire the gun yourself with each throw. In fact, once he accepts gunfire right next to himself, the extra conditioning may not be necessary. He may accept gunfire from anywhere.

Playing a gunfire conditioning tape while the pup fetches and feeds is the modern way to avoid gun-shyness.

May be important: Even when a retriever has been conditioned against gun-shyness by the tape, I'd go through the approaching gun sequence. I wouldn't be as cautious, perhaps, and I wouldn't move along as slowly as I've described in the early part of this step, but I'd do it to make sure this is all coming together properly in the dog's mind.

Step 18

Boat and Blind

The steadying we started in *Step 16* is hard on some dogs – especially those less than 8 months old. And then we had to enforce practicing straight lines and blind retrieves. We don't want to follow that stress with another tough exercise, so let's go back to something all well-bred retrievers love: water. Duke has been retrieving in water, and swimming just fine, but he hasn't learned about boats and blinds.

Start boat work in very shallow water.

With boat grounded, Duke won't be spooked by the unstable feeling of floating on water, especially when making his leap.

Getting into a grounded boat feels safer, too.

Of course, who can blame Duke if the first time out he decides to dip a pinkie in the water to see if it's too cold to jump in.

Start where the boat can be grounded in water just inches deep. SIT-STAY Duke on one of the boat seats. Throw a dummy, and send him. Our dog has had plenty of water experience, so it's no big deal for him to jump and splash after the dummy. The boat is grounded, so he probably won't even notice the feeling of unstable footing that a small boat usually imparts. Before moving into a little deeper water where Duke may get this wobbly feeling, give him three or four more retrieves so he comes to understand that the boat is safe.

Show Duke how to get in a boat until he catches on.

Help him in whatever way necessary at first.

Give the dog a little assistance by the collar or let him brace his neck against your hand.

Duke probably isn't used to climbing onto anything to deliver a dummy, but he does know GET IN. Lift his front feet to the gunwale of the boat, put your hand behind his head where it joins the neck, and say GET IN. He'll brace against your hand in order to raise his hind legs to the gunwale, and in he'll come. Help him each time, even in shallow water, because he should learn this now. When you're in deep water, your help will be a necessity.

Gradually work out to deeper water. At first, he'll just splash water on his body and face. Eventually, he's up to his chin before his feet hit bottom. And finally, he actually goes under for a moment because his feet never do touch bottom. It should cause no apprehension if you work into it slowly.

If you plan to hunt from a boat, you're ready for it. If you'll hunt from a blind, it's a good idea for Duke to know what that's like ahead of time, too.

Use a cardboard box to teach your dog how to leave the hole in a duck blind.

Start with a throw just outside the hole in the box, then increase the distance.

Your dog will learn this swiftly because the lesson takes advantage of the dog's natural inclination to take the shortest path. He sees the dummy through the hole, and it probably doesn't even occur to him to go around the box.

If the blind will have a hole from which Duke watches and marks falls, then leaps out to make the retrieve, you can simulate it with a hole cut in a large cardboard box. SIT-STAY him in the box and right behind the hole. Toss a dummy barely through the hole, and send him. He sees it, and it's so close that he's sure to go through the hole instead of trying to run around the outside of the box to fetch. Gradually lengthen the throw until he's leaving the hole and entering water to make retrieves.

If you have a different blind set-up, try to simulate your arrangements. And, of course, if your blind is already built, simply use that for practice.

Step 19

Lines and Blinds in Water

As on land, we have two ways of teaching dogs to take straight lines on water. Obviously, we can't use the ground cable, but the other systems work on windless days.

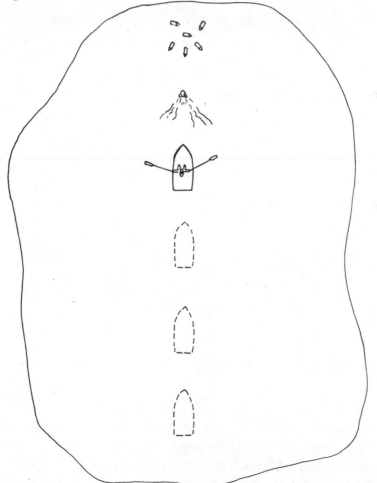

Back off farther with each retrieve to teach Duke to take straight lines in water.

We can row out with the dog in the boat and let him watch us drop a cluster of dummies. Then we back off, and send the dog from the boat while he can still easily see the dummies. After that, we row farther and farther away from the dummies for each retrieve. Duke knows where they are, so he swims in a straight line to get them.

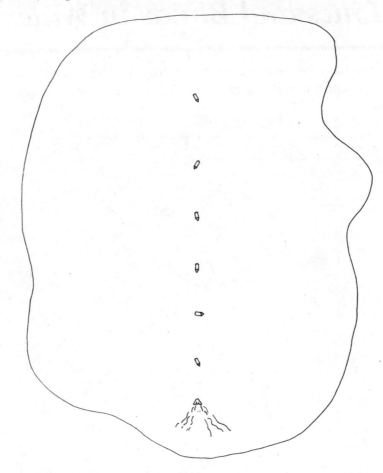

If there's no wind to spoil the line of dummies, this is an equally good method to teach straight lines in water.

Or we can drop the first dummy where it's easily visible from shore. The next one is farther out, but can be seen when Duke is fetching Number 1. Number 3 can be seen when he's retrieving Number 2, and so on. If wind drift doesn't spoil our sequence, our dog will have a good idea where the dummies are, and will swim a straight line to get them.

Important: The dog should have had much practice on shore so that running straight lines is already a habit before you try to make him take straight lines in water.

Equally important: Don't forget to always send the dog with the hand signal past his face so he is accustomed to taking direction to make that straight line.

The dog starts on command, doesn't see the dummy, then stops and looks back for clearer instructions.

This "popping" reaction is bad news when you're trying to send Duke for a crippled duck.

There's a problem with teaching blind retrieves. You've probably noticed it on land. It's called popping – probably for want of a better word – because the dog really never pops, he stops. You try to give him a line with the hand signal. He's accustomed to going with that signal, so he starts. One jump later it dawns on him that he doesn't see the dummy out there; he doesn't remember the dummy being dropped out there, and he didn't see a throw. Confused, he stops and looks back, either to see the throw or to get some hint of what he should do.

Popping can be bad news in the duck blind. With all our precautions to keep hidden from the ducks, we also often make it impossible for Duke to see many of the falls. A duck is down but swimming away, while Duke doesn't want to go because he doesn't know where it is. On top of that, maybe he stops to look back precisely when he should have been looking forward to mark another duck your buddy just dropped.

The old solution to this was to hide a buddy with a dummy somewhere across the water. You try to send Duke, and he makes that first jump. This is where he'd pop, but before he can do it, your buddy tosses the dummy to get Duke's attention. After some practice at this, it sinks through to Duke that he can have faith in you. Despite not seeing the throw, and not knowing where dummies were dropped, he can go when you command and be assured that, yes, there's a dummy out there to be fetched.

Problems! You don't always have a buddy to help. Also, those first throws should be close to get Duke started, but then Duke knows where the buddy is and starts watching for *his* throws instead of relying only on your commands.

It would be much better if we could send Duke without a throw at all. The dummy should just appear magically on the surface of the water just as Duke makes his first jump. Well, doggone if the dog training genius of Mayo Kellogg didn't produce exactly that situation by inventing an underwater dummy release.

Mayo Kellogg's underwater dummy release. If completely loaded like this, because of the buoyancy, it should be staked to the bottom.

Mayo's dummy release is a frame that holds several dummies. A bar holds them in place. When the heavy frame is sunk, a cord back to the trainer is used to pull the bar off the first dummy, and up it comes. The other dummies are released one after the other in the same manner in the spot near the shore or blind in order to give Duke repetitious practice.

Start by releasing a dummy before the FETCH command, so the dog can see it.

That one's easy.

Then pop one or two up immediately after the command and before the dog "pops."

Once the dog believes there will always be a dummy, dummies can be released when he's farther and farther out.

It doesn't take long for the dog to learn that when you give him a line, there will indeed be a dummy out there to fetch. After that, the dummies aren't released during Duke's first jump. We can wait until he hits water, then until he's swimming, and finally until he's almost to the dummy before letting it pop to the surface. Following that, we move the release frame farther and farther out so Duke learns no matter where you send him, if he goes in a straight line in that direction, there will be a dummy. For great distance, you will need a buddy hidden across a cove somewhere to pull the cord and release the dummies.

It's time to work Duke farther and farther onto land across the ditch.

Praise him highly for success, but never until the delivery is finished.

Now that Duke is taking straight lines on both land and water, let's go back to the ditch where we practiced during an earlier session. We only had him fetch dummies from on the opposite shore. He's ready now to make retrieves from farther and farther onto that opposite shore and even make some blind retrieves on dummies we plant over there before the session.

Step 20

Serious Obedience

If you took your dog from step to step as fast as he'd accept training without pressure, he could be five or six months old. That's young for serious obedience because the pressure becomes more intense. Watch for signs of the dog wilting. Ease up immediately if you notice it. You don't want to lose any of the gains you've made. Before returning the dog to his kennel, go through a few simple things he's good at, and end the session in the spirit of play with uncomplicated retrieves and lots of praise.

Duke may have accepted training more slowly, or your lack of time could have delayed it. No problem. Nothing to be ashamed of, either. But if he's eight to 12 months old, you have to be aware that, somewhere in this period, training will be complicated by his natural urge to test your authority. Remember Steve Rafe's method of gaining control over the dog, which is detailed in *Part 1, Step 9,* and use it as often as necessary. With Rafe's system you won't have to be nearly as tough with Duke. More importantly, when the two of you are through this phase, your previously excellent rapport will still be intact.

There's also a chance, of course, that you didn't acquire Duke as a puppy and couldn't do all the play training. You could even have a fully mature dog that barely knows his name. Become friends before you try Rafe's control methods. Be the person who feeds him for at least two weeks. Talk to him every time you go past. Pet him a lot. A large, mature—and *afraid*—dog can be difficult, and dangerous, to handle. When he has learned to trust you, control is more easily accepted.

If Duke has progressed rapidly, you may be tempted to ignore serious obedience. He's obeying, you say—what more could you ask!

Most of Duke's obedience has been voluntary because we made it fun and advantageous for him to obey. Now it's time to add a new element—MUST—to Duke's understanding. If we don't, there will come a time when obeying us is clearly less fun and advantageous than something else he'd rather be doing just then. We're out of control when Duke decides to chase a feral cat through a cornfield, wildly flushing the pheasants you drove 50 miles to hunt. And we're out of control when Duke breaks skim ice for the first time, is spooked by the experience, and decides it's more fun and advantageous to lounge on the floor of the blind rather than to retrieve this particular duck.

We're also about ready to introduce birds. When Duke switches from dummies to the real thing, the big change could inspire a rather creative response. Delivering a dummy was one thing, but this *bird—wow!* "It's mine! I found it, didn't I? Waddya mean COME? I gotta find a place to bury this thing!"

OK, you're willing to teach Duke that there are no options in obeying commands. From now on, MUST goes with every order. Maybe you consider joining an obedience class. Your neighbor's collie learned really fast in his class. Don't. While obedience classes are excellent, they're not the best for hunting retrievers. The SIT-STAY in obedience class is routinely broken with COME. As we've said before, we want our dog to know SIT-STAY means "stay put until you return or until further notice," not "wait anxiously to break with the COME command." We will violate our own rule, but only occasionally, not on a regular basis.

If Duke likes to forge ahead, do an about-face.

When he's brought up short by the leash a few times . . .

. . . he'll learn to avoid the discomfort by staying in position where he can pay close attention to your movements.

We'll use the choke chain again. Be sure to install it properly. We need to jerk and release. Remember? Installed backward, the chain keeps choking. (See *Part 1, Step 17* if you've forgotten.)

Let's start with HEEL. It's quite possible that Duke is so good at this that he won't seem to need further discipline. If so, set up temptations. It's temptations that eventually give us trouble if we fail to teach Duke he must do as we say.

If Duke always likes to forge ahead during HEEL, give him a chance to do it now. Start at a brisk walk, then slow down. He may continue at the same pace and leave you. If he does, do an about-face and be moving forcefully in the opposite direction when Duke hits the end of the leash or check cord. A few rude awakenings like this, and Duke begins to pay better attention.

Duke has always walked at HEEL. Now vary the speed.

Change speeds radically now. Run. Walk. Jog. Change directions sharply and frequently. Reverse direction. Duke hits the choke chain, or you jerk it, each time he fails to pay attention to whatever you do, or fails to stay at your side. As before, we want Duke *near* our side, but not bumping our legs.

HEEL training isn't complete until Duke does it well in the presence of considerable distractions.

When Duke seems to be perfect at HEEL, go to the park or whatever place you know will have strange people and dogs. HEEL Duke among these distractions, at first just normal walking HEEL, but switching to changes in speed and direction when he begins to ignore the dogs and people. Again, whenever Duke forgets he's with you, do an about-face and wake him up.

SIT-STAY must also be practiced among distractions.

Practice SIT-STAY among distractions as soon as Duke is reliable at HEEL. Keep him on the check cord at first. HEEL a short distance near other people and dogs, then SIT-STAY him. If, or when, he's reliable, you can leave Duke and walk off farther than the length of the check cord, but continue to use it in case you need to catch him.

You were always in sight during SIT-STAY. Now tempt him to break by hiding.

Now comes the supreme SIT-STAY test. Duke has remained at SIT-STAY under a variety of conditions ranging from just beside you to way beyond the length of the check cord from you, maybe even 50 yards or more. But you were always in sight, and according to what he has been led to believe, could always enforce the command. Now you will disappear behind a tree or bush. This is important, because one day you may need to leave Duke and stalk within range of ducks on your belly.

How Duke reacts to this depends much on his personality. Some dogs are pretty sure they no longer have to obey this command. Others become anxious and feel the need to come looking for you. Don't go far before disappearing. And peek around to keep him in view. If he moves, and he probably will, step out and raise hell. Take him back where he had been. SIT-STAY him again, and disappear once more. Repeat until Duke is reliable, then increase the distance you go before disappearing. Gradually wait longer and longer before returning to the dog.

If Duke is a real problem about SIT-STAY with you out of sight, use a check cord. Add a choke collar if necessary.

If your dog is a real problem, loosely loop the check cord around a sapling near the dog (around a pre-driven stake, if necessary) then take the long end of the cord with you and disappear behind cover. When he moves, jerk hard and prove to him that you still have control.

Caution: Do this disappearing act without distraction at first. Practice it around people and other dogs only after he's very reliable about staying put.

You can tap the rear of a reluctant sitter with a broomstick.

Some dogs hate the SIT command worse than any other and will try to delay responding in the hope that you'll forget it completely, only sitting after being angrily ordered. Mayo Kellogg likes to use a broomstick to tap the dog on the rump if he fails to obey quickly enough. Later, you'll be hunting the dog with a shotgun, the barrel of which somewhat resembles the broomstick, so you'll always have the reminder along. Good Speed-Training trick! And indeed, the shotgun can be used just like the broomstick to tap the dog.

I rattle the stick between his legs if he's slow to sit.

My version of using a stick (broomstick, limb, or whatever is handy) some-times works even faster. If Duke doesn't sit instantly, I rattle the stick between his hind legs. Be careful. You're in the vicinity of tender parts. Duke is also aware of this danger and sits promptly.

For the dog that really hates to obey SIT, touching the anal area sometimes works.

Some dogs are slow to sit even with stick rattling between their legs. For this dog, just touch, *do not tap* the anal or genitals with the stick. Few dogs fail to squat quickly to protect themselves.

Whether rattling or touching, do it immediately after a sharp SIT command. If Duke sits instantly, he escapes the reminder. If he's not quick about it, he doesn't.

For the dog that hates SIT, start making him do it before every enjoyable activity: eating, getting in the car, whatever. He may learn to love the command.

Practice COME in the presence of distractions by using it with the FETCH routine instead of breaking SIT-STAY with COME.

The COME command has been used so much during retrieving that it's strongly imbedded in Duke's psyche. Continue to practice it that way instead of breaking SIT-STAY with COME, saving that particular release for only special occasions. If Duke is contrary about COME at his current age, Speed-Train his response with the choke chain and practice in the presence of other people and dogs.

This is one of the few times we break SIT-STAY with COME.

Some dogs dawdle on COME, which presents us with a second special occasion to break SIT-STAY with COME. The first time, we used it to improve Duke's water entry. This time place the dog at SIT-STAY and walk off 100 yards or more. Make him wait until he can't stand the suspense and fears he's left behind forever. When you order COME, ol' Duke the Dawdler will close the gap in high gear. Repeat as necessary to maintain the dog's quick response, but don't make a habit of breaking SIT-STAY with COME.

Step 21

Birds

At long last, the birds! Why so late? Because there are so many things best accomplished with dummies, and some young dogs will hardly touch a dummy once they've handled the real thing. Our Speed-Trained dogs are so well indoctrinated in fetching dummies that nearly all will continue to handle them with enthusiasm.

Oddly enough, while some dogs feel dummies are kid stuff once they've fetched birds, others have trouble making the transition from dummies to birds. The dummy odors are familiar, they connect those odors with retrieving, and they don't immediately grasp that they should also fetch this odd thing that not only smells and tastes somewhat different – it *feels* different! Don't worry. If Duke does that, we'll correct it with Mayo Kellogg's hat trick.

Your dog may not immediately grab its first bird.

Start with a dead pigeon. Toss it for a simple retrieve. If Duke runs out and sniffs, but doesn't immediately grab it, don't get excited. And keep your mouth shut so you don't distract him away from it. Let him study it if he wants. He'll probably remember what he's there for and will eventually fetch it.

If not, fetch it yourself. Run out there enthusiastically. Kneel down, your nose close to the bird. Scratch in the grass beside it. Duke will come running to find out what interests you so much. Pick up the bird, and carry it back to the starting point. Toss it again. Very likely, Duke will take your example and fetch it this time.

Kellogg's hat (cap) trick will convince Duke to fetch his first bird.

Should this fail, toss his favorite dummy a couple times, then switch back to the dead pigeon. Try this routine several times. He'll probably make the switch.

If not, it's time for Kellogg's hat trick. Remember when we had you use a sock or sweat-scented first dummy because we promised that later your scent could effect a cure? Now is the time. Mayo places the pigeon in his cap, holds it all together with a rubber band, and tries another toss. The bird now smells more like Mayo's scent, and almost invariably his dog retrieves it. Duke is accustomed to his master's scent on nearly everything he handles, and now the bird seems more "normal." After a few fetches, the cap can be removed, and the dog probably won't notice the difference.

If Mayo doesn't happen to have a cap and rubber band handy, he ties his handkerchief around the bird and gets the same results.

Bonus: Your cap or knotted handkerchief is also a great substitute dummy that can be used to "jolly" your dog back out of a wilt when something goes wrong. Maybe a hunting buddy blasts a barrage right over Duke's head, convincing Duke that the only safe place is behind your heels. Retrieving is his fun game, and your scent on the cap or handkerchief means "safe and familiar" to the dog. A few tosses will usually erase his terrors. *But do it immediately.* Don't wait and let him think about his new fear until it gets stuck in his head. If for some reason you can't jolly him out of it right away, don't put him back in the same circumstance that caused this fear for at least the next two weeks. Give the memory a chance to fade before risking it again.

Scott's pigeon harness is an economical and effective way to plant birds.

When Duke is retrieving dead pigeons without problems, substitute live pigeons for the feather dummies during quartering/searching practice. Plant the pigeons with Scott's Velcro fastened restraint harnesses for Speed-Train results. (Buy the ones with attached release cords; we'll use them later.) These harnesses cost very little and are more effective in this particular training step than are the rather expensive bird-release cages.

Let the dog find a harnessed pigeon just inside heavy cover.

At this point, flushing is unnecessary. You plant the harnessed birds, and they stay right there — unlike a certain percentage of pigeons when they're just dizzied and planted. (Dizzied pigeons alert quickly but tend to stay put except late in the day when they are eager to return to the roost. If you train after work in the evening, harnesses are extra important.) The dog searches in his hunting pattern, finds the harnessed pigeons, and retrieves them just like he used to fetch dummies.

But, you say, that's not training a dog to flush game, that's retrieving practice. True, but think about it. When you take him hunting, he'll be searching for those harnessed pigeons. When he finds wild birds instead, I guarantee you they'll flush. Presto! Duke is now a Speed-Trained flush dog.

Another bonus to all this is the fact that Duke is learning that you take him where the birds are. It makes him more attentive and willing to quarter near you.

While some dogs are shy of birds at first, others don't care to share them.

While some dogs are feather shy at first, others are quite the opposite. Work the dog on the check cord until you learn he won't try to run off with these new prizes. If he does try to claim the pigeons, give him Steve Rafe's control treatment, and run the dog through the serious obedience sequence, allowing no sloppy, half-hearted work. A reminder with a slingshot is also useful if the dog tries to run off with the bird. (See *Part 2, Step 1* for details.)

If the dog thinks he's controlled, he's controlled.

After that, run him in search practice with the short cord attached to make him think you still control him with the check cord. He won't look back to check its length.

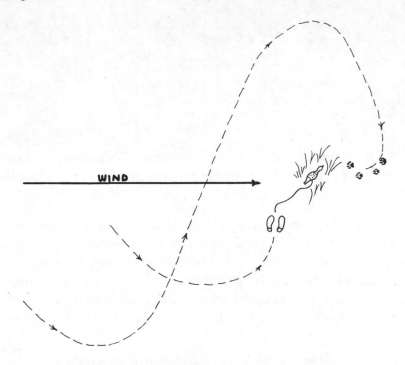

This maneuver gets you to the pigeon first. When the dog catches its scent, pull the cord to free the wing strap and launch the bird.

When Duke is retrieving planted pigeons successfully, bring him with the wind toward one of the birds so he won't smell it in advance. Have your shotgun along. Guide him (with the check cord, if necessary) into making a swing away from the pigeon so you can get to the bird first. Grab the harness cord, and give the long whistle to turn Duke back toward you. When he catches the scent and rushes in, jerk the cord which pulls the velcro fastener free and launches the pigeon all in one motion. If your timing is perfect, the bird will be released just far enough ahead of the dog that it doesn't get caught. Let the pigeon get some distance and altitude so you won't hit Duke, who is surely chasing, then kill the bird for him to retrieve.

Now you have a hunter. Shoot a few more pigeons for Duke, and he'll be ready for his first season. He'll have no trouble switching from pigeons to game birds. Many hunters are satisfied with a dog trained just this far.

Plant a clay bird launcher to simulate the flush.

If you don't have, and can't get, enough pigeons to kill a few more, fake it with your clay-bird thrower. Save the dead pigeon. Keep it frozen, but thaw it before each training session. Plant live harnessed birds on the course as before. And let Duke retrieve them as before. But for the "kill," plant your clay-bird thrower. (Change its location every session.) Place the dead pigeon away from the thrower in the direction the clay bird will sail.

Duke may wince with surprise the first time the trap throws a clay bird.

But when he learns it means a fetch, he'll love the commotion it makes.

When you get close to the clay-bird thrower, whistle Duke toward you, trip the cord, and shoot the clay bird. Give the dog a line just downwind of the pigeon for a blind retrieve, and he'll fetch the dead bird you've planted. In addition, the thrower will condition your dog to the idea of a commotion occurring before a shot—as when a covey of quail bursts out, or a cackling pheasant takes to the air. And you'll Speed-Train the dog with some extra shooting practice before the season. If the first experience shakes the dog, do the "jollying retrieves" stunt with your cap or handkerchief.

If you like, and if Duke is tendermouthed, you can substitute a harnessed live pigeon for the dead bird.

Important: Plant the harnessed pigeons just inside cover at first—like a small patch of high weeds or maybe just a clump of grass that's taller than the rest of the pasture. The fact that Duke finds birds where cover is heavier than average for the area teaches him to look for and hunt that sort of cover. This is especially important for dogs that are a bit lazy and would rather run around the heavy stuff instead of getting in there and searching. As Duke learns where to hunt, plant the pigeons deeper and deeper into heavy cover. Make him work for his pigeons, and he'll search much harder for wild birds later.

Step 22

Hunting Short

While shooting pigeons for Duke, or when sending him for planted blinds after clay-bird throws, you may be frustrated by his hunting short. He runs out in the direction sent, but goes only about as far as you'd ordinarily toss a dummy. We tried to Speed-Train past this problem the first time we used the ground cable. We tried to teach Duke to keep going until he smells the bird, regardless of the distance. If he is failing to use his nose now, go back to the cable. He hasn't had enough practice.

He's ready? OK, now we'll enhance Duke's enthusiasm for marking and searching by using pigeons instead of scented or feathered dummies. The real thing is always more exciting. (Had we done this earlier, however, some dogs would have lost interest in fetching dummies, which complicates the training process.)

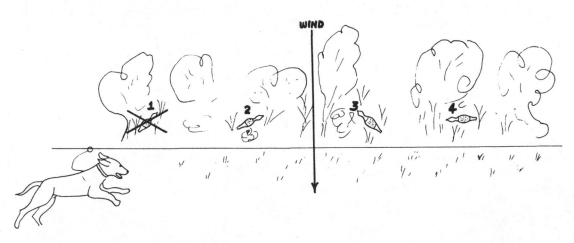

This set-up with cable, pigeons, and correct wind direction will correct the dog that habitually hunts short.

Stake the cable along the downwind edge of cover. Make sure the first pigeon is planted so close that Duke can't hunt short. Plant two more at 15- or 20-foot intervals. He'll almost certainly go that far to make a blind search. If not, shorten the intervals. Use a longer chain or dropper cable so Duke can reach the birds in the cover, of course.

When Duke is reliably fetching blinds at these distances, discontinue the Number 1 bird and place it as Number 4. When he's accustomed to that, discontinue Number 2 and place it as Number 5. Keep this up until Duke is fetching blinds the full length of the cable. He'll probably keep checking those first discontinued positions, but he'll gradually learn that there always may be another bird farther out if he just keeps searching.

Work a cover edge to extend your dog's searching range.

Be sure the wind will blow the bird scent toward your dog.

To add more distance to Duke's blind searches, discontinue the cable, but keep working along a fence row or edge of a hayfield—anywhere there is a cover edge next to an easy place to run. Now you can gradually extend his range to 300 yards or more. A gliding duck, goose, or pheasant can make a long retrieve. By now you can probably speed the process by increasing the distance between planted pigeons to perhaps 30 feet, or whatever the dog will take. Then increase the intervals gradually to 50 feet, or even more if Duke is a fast learner.

Step 23

Hardmouth

Another reason we waited so long to switch from dummies to birds was to give Duke long conditioning in carrying softly. There's no incentive to chomp down on dummies, and we hoped that the light carry would become so deeply ingrained that we could Speed-Train right past the need for hardmouth correction. Some dogs, however, will succumb anyhow. The strong scent, the feel of flesh, and the taste of blood is too much. This is no dummy: This is lunch!

Gag him by pushing the bird farther into his mouth. He'll release.

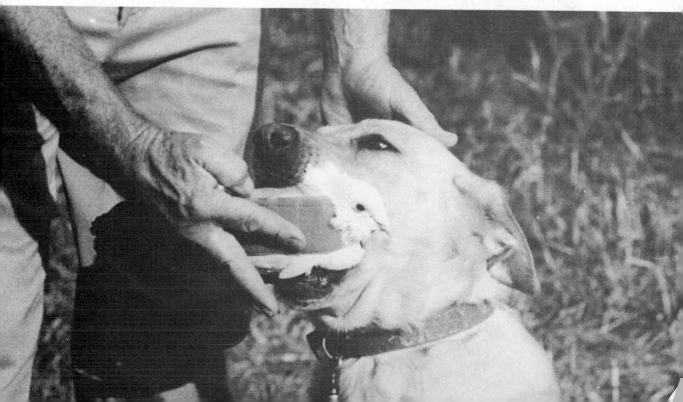

Nip this hardmouth in the bud. The quickest method involves a slight risk, so you may want to try the safer methods first. The mildest is a simple "no." Toss the dead pigeon on the ground, say FETCH, and when Duke hardmouths it, say no. If he lets up, fine. If not, shove it farther into his mouth to gag him and make him release the bird.

Important: The no is not "NO!" but no as in "nope." We don't want to yell at Duke and give him the notion that fetching birds is wrong.

Repeat the fetch several times, saying no and withholding praise if he chomps. When he does hold the pigeon lightly, praise Duke lavishly before taking the bird with GIVE.

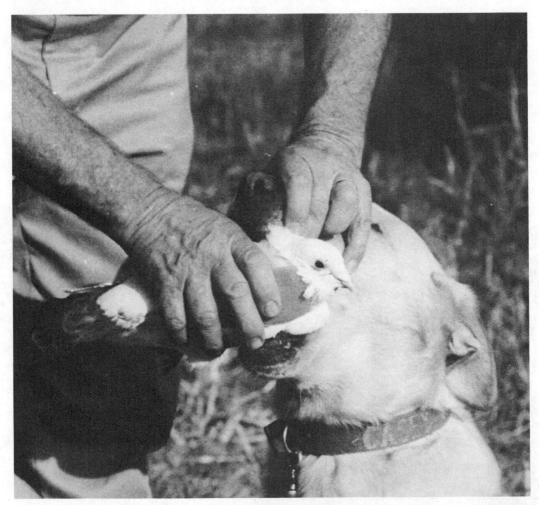

Push the upper lips over the fangs as you insert the bird.

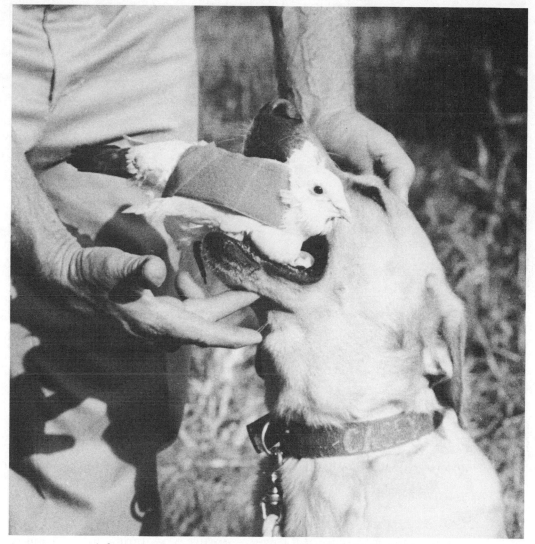

A finger under the chin makes him hold the bird as placed.

The quiet "no" didn't work? OK, we'll have to make it a little more uncomfortable for Duke to chomp. Pull his lips over his fangs, say FETCH, and thrust the pigeon in Duke's mouth. Let him hold it. He won't chomp his own lips. Praise the light hold with GOOD FETCH instead of GOOD BOY. Press your middle or index finger under the dog's chin so he can't spit it out. When he accepts the idea (probably after several tries), HEEL him and make him carry the pigeon with his lips over his fangs.

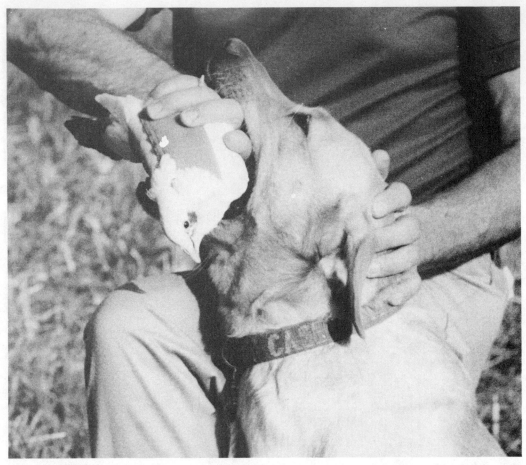

At your own risk, roll your hand into the dog's mouth as you insert the pigeon.

My favorite method works much faster for me but involves a slight risk. It's not as dangerous as it looks, but if you're unsure of your dog, or have a very low pain threshold, don't try it. Dog trainers don't even think about it as a risk, but amateurs might. What I'm saying is I don't want to hear about it if Duke pinches your pinkie. You're on your own.

Grasp the dead pigeon firmly in your hand with the bird's head hanging loose. Shake it in front of Duke's nose so the smell and motion of the wobbling head makes the dog grab. As he grabs, simply roll your hand so it enters Duke's mouth before the bird. If Duke chomps down the slightest, howl *"ouch! easy!"* Sound mortally wounded. Few dogs will bite the hand that feeds them, and they soon learn to soften the grip.

Blunted, shortened roofing nails will make hardmouthing uncomfortable, but not painful.

I don't care for this method, but I include it for those who don't want their hand in a dog's mouth. Shorten and blunt several roofing nails and shove them through adhesive tape. I repeat: *shortened and blunted* roofing nails. The idea is not to inflict pain, but to make it uncomfortable for Duke to hardmouth the bird. Wrap the tape around the bird, and toss it for an ordinary retrieve. Use this for all retrieving until Duke loses his urge to chomp.

Step 24

Ducks

Dogs will switch easily from pigeons to upland birds of all kinds, but pigeons do not swim. We can shoot pigeons over water, and Duke can fetch them, but it doesn't teach him that ducks paddle off to hide in the marsh grass.

Rope was used to better illustrate how to shackle a duck, but the square knots hold better if strips of cloth are used instead.

Acquire a duck of either wild or domestic variety. They're messy, sloppy creatures to have around, but you won't have to keep a duck long. Shackle both wings and feet the first time you show it to Duke. You don't want him smacked on the nose by a wing on his first introduction.

The duck should go in the dog's mouth breast first.

Show the duck to Duke, then say FETCH, and put it in his mouth with your hand going in first to make sure he doesn't chomp down and hardmouth or kill it. Position the duck so Duke is holding it as it should be carried—by the body, not the neck, wings, or feet. If he's tendermouthed, withdraw your hand. With your finger under his chin, if necessary, make him hold it a minute while you pour on the praise.

Toss the shackled duck into the water for a few retrieves. SIT-STAY him, and make him hold until sent. Do several of these short sessions, but not more often than every other day.

Let Duke watch the duck walk off into the water and swim away.

Next, keep the wings shackled, but untie the legs. Place Duke on SIT-STAY. Let the duck walk into the water and swim away while you and Duke watch. Send the dog while the duck is still in sight. Don't overtire the duck by swimming it more than twice each session, but do several of these in-sight retrieving sessions.

Finally, let the duck swim out of sight before sending Duke, so he has to use his nose.

If you have time, and can tolerate the duck around the place a little while longer, you may want to give Duke a few lessons on what ducks can *really* be like. Clip the primary feathers (the long ones) on one wing so the duck can't fly, then free it in the water without shackles. Give the duck a head start, then send Duke to fetch this bird that can now slap and dive in order to escape. It's great practice and great exercise to get Duke ready for hunting season. It may get so exciting for the dog that he'll talk you into keeping the duck.

Part II

The Finished Dog

We've come a long way—swiftly for some, gradually for others. It doesn't matter. What does matter is that we started the pup early, so he has learned to learn and is now willing and able to grasp whatever a new situation has to offer or teach.

It's up to us whether we stop here and go on. The majority of amateur trainers quit long before this point. Some were satisfied with a partly trained dog, others found they couldn't devote even a few minutes a day to training, and many simply lacked the will to persist. Those who have taken their canines through every step in *Part I* already have better trained hunting dogs than most hunters they'll see in the field. But for those who can, there are good reasons to carry on until they have a finished dog:

1. We have introduced handling, which is guiding the dog to a fall by hand and whistle signals. Up close, Duke may enter cover as directed, or even accept help to guide him toward a dummy or bird. But if a duck falls at a distance, the only way we'll be able to guide Duke to it is by leading him there ourselves. And that, of course, is always when the sky starts to fill with waterfowl.

2. Duke will fetch a dead bird he was able to mark. But if the bird, perhaps a pheasant, hits the ground running, it's a maybe. Some dogs are natural retrievers. Others have no idea what to do if the bird isn't where they saw it

fall. And nearly all dogs — the good, poor, and in-between — are vastly improved by teaching them to use their noses.

3. Duke is a natural retriever. He retrieves because he loves it. But he doesn't know that he MUST do it. So what happens? One day, when confronted by a new situation, he decides he'd rather not. This time, fetching the duck doesn't seem worth the trouble. You can swim out there yourself, or lose perhaps the one bird you'll shoot all day. Force training doesn't sound nice. It even involves discomfort. But it's easier than you've heard. The dog himself chooses how long he's willing to accept the discomfort, and you end up with a dog that goes every time he's sent.

4. And then there are those seemingly uncanny canine moves that will amaze your friends into thinking you are the world's foremost trainer. A cripple and two dead birds drop out of a flock or covey. Your dog unfailingly goes for the cripple — on land or water! The pheasants or Western quail are running today. Your dog circles and herds them back.

Ready to go on?

Step 1

Sit Anywhere with Whistle

At the heart of handling is the dog's willingness to obey the single blast whistle command for SIT no matter where he is. Once he sits, he'll look to you for what comes next. If he doesn't sit, he won't be watching for hand signals.

Duke knows both voice and whistle commands for SIT. And we've devised insistent means for making sure he does it promptly. Now we have to convince Duke that he must also obey SIT at a distance from us.

The coonhunter's training rod.

Start with the training rod. It's just a 10-foot length of electrical conduit with one end smashed to accept the swivel end of a snap. A hole is drilled for a bolt which holds the snap securely. I borrowed this idea from the coonhound trainers. They use the rod to lead a coon through the woods to lay a trail for the hounds to follow. Because the coon must always walk a rod-length to the side, the hounds do not learn that it's easier to follow their master's trail than to follow the coon. We, of course, use it to make Duke sit anywhere as far as a rod-length away.

The training rod teaches our dog he must obey SIT, even when not at our side.

Install the choke chain properly on Duke's neck, snap the training rod to the ring, and order HEEL. Chances are, you have already used the rod for HEEL training, so start with the familiar HEEL on the rod. Walk a short distance at HEEL, then order SIT and enforce the command with the rod and choke chain. Praise the dog, then release him with ALL RIGHT. Quickly now, when he's just a couple steps ahead, blow the short, sharp whistle blast for SIT. If he hesitates in the slightest, jerk back on the choke chain with the rod. It won't take much, because we've already drilled prompt SIT into Duke during *Part 1, Step 20.* The difference is that he now must learn to sit no matter where he is in relation to us. Practice a few minutes every other day, having Duke sit at distances varying from right in front of you to a full 10 feet away.

With the rod, practice SIT at every conceivable angle and distance possible.

When Duke is responding promptly, make a change. Do the HEEL, SIT, ALL RIGHT, DISTANCE SIT routine once, but don't put Duke back on HEEL. Just release him from the DISTANCE SIT with ALL RIGHT, and start walking at the same moment. As Duke walks forward with you, turn as you stride ahead so he's positioned off to your left side instead of to the front. If necessary, manage him with the rod. Blast SIT with the whistle, and enforce it with the rod.

Release him again and turn as you walk so Duke is on your right. Sit him again.

From this point on, forget HEEL during SIT training. Let the dog go where he will when released (within the length of the 10-foot rod, of course) and practice SIT at all possible distances as well as everywhere within the full 360 degrees around you.

Practice a few minutes every other day until Duke is responding instantly no matter where he is. If it takes two weeks, practice two more weeks to establish the habit.

SIT with distraction is enforceable with the rod.

Distraction training progresses fastest if you start with a pup doing the pestering. A grown dog can ignore a pup. Keep the stronger distractions—mature dogs are competition—for later in the training.

Distraction time. Bring in somebody with a strange dog or cat as you whistle SIT. Enforce it. Take Duke to the park to practice where there are numbers of people. Again, if it takes two weeks of training to control Duke in the midst of distractions, practice that much longer.

Duke's not obeying SIT at a distance beyond 10 feet? Drive a staple stake over the training cable.

Duke is now very familiar with the notion that he obeys SIT at a distance. But what distance? He has been trained up to 10 feet. He may not obey beyond that. Time for cable training again.

U-shaped, or staplelike, stakes come with the cable. It's best to order at least five of them so you'll have two for each end when the soil is soft. Drive the extra one into the ground, straddling the cable at its mid-point.

Start with a retrieve just short of the staple.

You should've also ordered two short dropper cables with rings to slide up and down the ground cable. If not, make up a short chain with a ring on one end and a snap on the other so you'll have a dropper on each end of the cable. Duke can only go as far as the mid-point stake with either dropper. Snap the dog to one of the droppers with the choke chain instead of the collar, place him on SIT about 10 feet (he's used to that distance) from the mid-point stake. Toss a dummy at or near the stake where Duke can reach it. Have him fetch.

Whistle SIT just as the dropper ring is about to hit the staple.

If he doesn't obey, it's, "Whoops, I should have."

"I will next time."

Now, still standing 10 feet from the mid-point stake, toss the dummy well beyond the stake so there's no way Duke can get far enough past the stake to reach it. Blow the *tweet-tweet* for FETCH (the dog also knows it as GO) then, just as the dropper ring nears the stake, blow the sharp blast for SIT. If Duke thinks he's off the training rod and believes he doesn't have to obey instantly, he'll get an emphatic correction when the ring hits the stake and sharply jerks the choke chain. He'll stop quicker next time.

Fetch the dummy yourself, and drop it just in front of the dog with him at SIT-STAY.

Command FETCH, and trill COME as the dog grabs the dummy.

Duke is probably on SIT now. If not, SIT him near the stake where he should have obeyed the whistle command. Go pick up the dummy yourself, and return to your starting point. Turn the dog around if he isn't already facing you. Toss the dummy midway between you and the dog. Whistle FETCH or GO (*tweet-tweet*) and just as Duke reaches for the dummy, blow the trill for COME, and point your arm straight down for the hand signal. Turn your left side to the dog, whistle SIT, and accept the dummy.

As Duke learns to SIT on command in the middle of a retrieve, back off from the staple stake to increase the distance.

From now on, practice with a cord attached to the dummy. The dummy is always tossed or carried out of reach beyond the stake, but when Duke sits as commanded, you can pick up the cord and pull the dummy within his reach as you order FETCH. Begin at 10 feet, then gradually back off so that Duke learns he must obey SIT regardless of the distance between you. Anytime the dog fails to obey, of course, he's jerked to a halt by his dropper cable ring hitting the stake.

Throughout this practice continue to use the down arm signal. Although he won't see it when he hears the COME whistle, he'll see it and get its message as he runs toward you.

Duke has always come all the way to you on the COME command.

Now stop him midway with the SIT whistle and a little help from a screw eye in a post.

Our dog also will have to learn to SIT while coming toward you if he is to be handled at a distance. Try it while he's coming toward you on the cable. Some dogs have learned SIT well enough by this time that they'll respond as desired. Others won't. They've always trotted all the way to you after the COME command, and they can't easily change the pattern. In fact, they probably think they *shouldn't* change the pattern.

If your dog has problems with stopping to SIT on the way to you, give the command just as he's about to be stopped by the stake anyway. An alternative method that allows you to stop Duke in a greater variety of locations requires a large screw-eye in a fence post. Run the check cord through the eye, leaving the snap on the short end. Attach Duke by his choke chain, back away about half the check cord length, whistle COME, and let the cord slide through the eye. When Duke is nearing you, blow SIT and grip the cord to bring him up short if he fails to obey.

Vary the distance at which Duke is ordered to SIT, and practice until he's doing it right every time. As usual, note how long this took, and practice that much longer.

If your dog is 8 to 12 months old, he may be making progress difficult by his notion that he, not you, should be in control. Give him some confinement punishment. Go back to Steve Rafe's top dog routine. If all else fails, read *Part 2, Step 11.*

You could grab Duke's collar and give him a good thrashing with a light limb, too, but avoid it if anything else will work. I'm no bleeding heart. I've straightened out the thinking of many dogs this way myself. Every time you have to resort to a thrashing, though, you've lost a piece of rapport that never entirely comes back.

If Duke is wise to training rod and check cord, try Mayo Kellogg's favorite arm extender—a slingshot.

When Duke SITS well to the whistle on check cord and cable, it's time for the big test. Will he obey when running free? Use the choke chain for this, because he associated wearing it with being controlled. Snap on the short 3-foot cord. He doesn't know the length and associates check cords with control.

With all this, he'll probably respond just as asked. But it's not wise to chance letting him get away with disobedience even once. If you have, or are willing to buy, a *pump*-type air pistol, use that to pop his rear if he disobeys. Pump it just enough to sting, not injure. Don't use a CO_2 pistol unless its velocity can be adjusted down to about the sting of a spring-driven Daisy BB gun. The BB gun would be perfect, of course, but I hesitate to correct with something that resembles a shotgun. The sight of the shotgun should signal fun, not fear.

A cheaper way out is Mayo Kellogg's favorite, the slingshot. Either buy or make one. (Inner tubes, though, no longer make good slingshots.) Practice with marbles against a target on an old sheet draped over a clothesline. That way you can recover the marbles.

If you don't become as good as Mayo, you might prefer bird shot to marbles. A pattern of shot from the slingshot is more likely to find its target, and poor aim will not ruin a promising stud dog.

Obviously, test the dog when he's near so you *can* hit his rump. He'll soon get the idea that even though he's running free, he must still obey.

Step 2

Over

To Duke, FETCH ordinarily has meant being sent from your side. But now he must learn to sit in front of you and take hand signals that guide him "over," either right or left, to the dummy. What happens? You seat Duke facing you, toss the dummy a few feet to one side where he can see it, then extend an arm in that direction as you blow the *tweet-tweet* on your whistle. Duke starts to go, then thinks that this can't be right, and runs to your side before making the retrieve, or perhaps sits at your side awaiting further instructions. How do you get Duke to make the transition from leaving your side to leaving from wherever he's sitting to make the retrieve? Here is where the cable really shines.

To teach OVER, SIT the dog in front instead of beside you . . .

... then send him with the FETCH whistle and lots of body English. Attach a short check cord if Duke needs control.

Attach Duke to the cable's dropper. Also snap a short check cord to his collar. (If he breaks and goes before he's sent, you'll be able to stop him and retrieve the dummy yourself. A few times of not getting to fetch will steady him.) Place the dog facing you and at SIT-STAY. In the beginning, stand in front of the dog. Throw the dummy a short distance. Simultaneously whistle FETCH, make one step in the direction you want him to go, and shoot your arm out in that direction.

Practice this in both directions until Duke is no longer breaking and is no longer acting confused about not being sent from your side. Because you're standing so close to the dog, he may never act confused, but practice close-up anyway so he learns to read your body motions.

As you practice, gradually move back from the dog before signaling FETCH.

Now comes the transition. Step back so the dropper prevents him from quite being able to reach you. Toss the dummy, and whistle FETCH accompanied by your usual body English. If he tries to swing out to your side before going, stop him, place him back on SIT-STAY, and fetch the dummy yourself. Don't let him retrieve until he goes straight for the dummy. Step forward when he goes so you'll be within his reach to make the delivery. Praise highly when he returns with the dummy.

Move back as far as possible while still being able to return to the cable in time to accept the dummy.

Once Duke gets the idea that the cable will stop him from getting to your side anyhow, and that if he tries it he won't get to fetch, you can begin stepping back farther and farther and throwing the dummy farther and farther. There will be a limit as to how far you can leave the cable, because you must have time to return while Duke is making the retrieve.

Practice until Duke will run straight down the cable, either right or left, and all the way to the end where you may have to plant dummies if you can't toss that far. However long this takes, practice another time that long.

Use a natural barrier such as a fence to help stop the dog when teaching OVER without cable restraint.

When you're satisfied that Duke is proficient enough to take OVER signals without the cable restraint, give it a try. Keep the short cord on him to maintain his illusion of being under control. If he performs as expected, throw or plant the dummies, then back off farther and farther before sending Duke to right or left. Now, of course, he can deliver all the way to you, so you won't have to step forward to accept the dummy.

At first, keep him working in the same familiar place while you back off. When he's good at that, you can move him to work in different places.

Finally, you can plant dummies in the field before going for walks. When in the vicinity, whistle SIT, then send him OVER to make the retrieve. At this time, however, because Duke still needs some work on being sent back, always arrange it so he can be stopped with SIT at a fence, then sent along the fence for his OVER command. This helps guide him and eliminates the need to send him in any direction but right or left.

Send Duke OVER with his check cord running through a screw-in stake-out.

Drop the cord to let him finish the retrieve.

If Duke fails when off the cable, perhaps because he knows he's unrestrained or because conditions are not quite the same, we'll go to another method to make the transition from cable to running free. Use one of the spiral or screw-type stake-outs. Twist it into the ground, then run a long check cord through the eye. You can also use a screw eye in a post, but the stake-out is better because later you can move it to new places and prevent one-location obedience.

Start Duke close to the stake-out. You have the long end of the cord. Send him OVER. If he comes toward you (which isn't likely with all the cable training), stop him with the cord. Fetch the dummy yourself, with Duke on SIT-STAY.

If he goes straight to the dummy, release the cord, let it slide through the eye, and whistle COME just as Duke reaches for the dummy. Duke can now bring the dummy to you without the need for you to step forward. For that reason, this is actually a more natural system than the cable, but the cable was much superior in teaching the dog that he can't come to your side before making the fetch.

Step 3

Back

We won't need a new, or another, signal for BACK. We taught our dog that *tweet-tweet* on the whistle means FETCH. We also used it to release the dog from SIT before the food bowl, to release in the field from SIT, GO OVER either right or left, and GO for blinds. By now, the signal means all of these things to Duke despite the fact that we need a separate name for each. How can this be? Simple. Duke has learned what he wants to do—which is what he has been taught to do, and what he now regards as fun. But he's also usually under a restraining command and can't do what he wants until he hears the whistle. The *tweet-tweet* has become simply a release meaning, "Go do what you're supposed to do."

Start BACK training with the dog on the cable with a short dropper. Have him face you at SIT-STAY.

To teach BACK, snap Duke to the short dropper, and SIT him at the end of the ground cable facing you. Toss a dummy over and several feet behind the dog, making sure it falls where he can reach it.

Prepare to send the dog with the up arm signal.

Send him with whistle and arm.

Add body motion for emphasis.

Blow the whistle for FETCH, GO, or whatever you choose to call it now, and simultaneously shoot your arm straight up for the BACK hand signal. Duke knows where the dummy landed and will whirl around to make the short retrieve. Gradually increase the length of throw as you practice. Finally, start planting dummies along the cable, throwing only the first one and having Duke retrieve the others as blinds. Each time, start with him facing you, and use the arm up signal.

Responding to BACK from a distance can be taught by sending Duke from the same place each time, but with you backing off farther with each retrieve.

With all Duke's past experience, it won't take long to become good at BACK. When he is, switch to starting him from midway on the cable. Plant the dummies behind him. At first, stand just a few feet away from him as you did when working from the end of the cable. After a few fetches, however, start moving back from the dog before sending him. Gradually move farther away with each retrieve until finally Duke is starting from midway and delivering to you at the end of the cable. You can even back off farther than the cable's end before sending the dog, but, of course, you'll have to return to the cable to accept the dummy. This is teaching Duke that he can, in fact *must*, react to the whistle and hand (really arm) signal for BACK no matter what the distance.

Try him off the cable occasionally, and remember how many sessions it took before he functioned as well off the cable as on. Practice that much longer off the cable.

Step 4

Handling

Duke knows that *tweet-tweet* on the whistle means GO, trill means COME, and there are four hand or arm signals. The arm goes down for COME IN, up for BACK, right arm out to go OVER that direction, and left arm out for the other. Now it's time to put it all together and completely handle the dog.

Duke can't shortcut the corner fence, so . . .

. . . he goes around it.

Start by making two 90-degree turns in the cable. How can a stake hold the cable at the turn, yet let the dog pass? It sounds hard, but it's easy. Build a little fence with a piece of plywood nailed onto two stakes driven into the ground in the inside corner of the cable. Drive the stakes first, then fasten the plywood. It's also a good idea to drive the stake nearest to the cable at a slight outward angle to ensure that the cable can't somehow ride upward. The fence will have to be long enough that it's apparent to the dog that he can't get around it by shortcutting the corner. The dog finds he must travel on the cable side of the fence, so the dropper ring slides around the corner with no problem, and the dog negotiates the corner with ease.

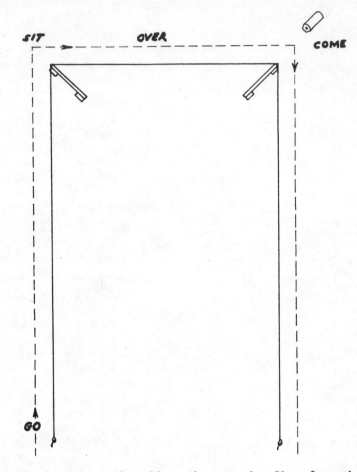

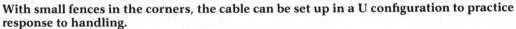

With small fences in the corners, the cable can be set up in a U configuration to practice response to handling.

With two corner fences, arrange the cable in a long U-shaped configuration. Stand at the end of one leg with Duke facing you. Send him BACK with the whistle and upraised arm. Just as the dropper ring reaches the corner where it will help stop the dog's momentum, blow SIT on the whistle.

When Duke sits and looks back to you for further direction, whistle again and extend your arm for OVER. The dog will find the dummy at just dropper length beyond the second corner. This pulls the ring onto the corner, ready to slide down the second leg of the cable. As Duke runs for the dummy, you hurry to the end of the second leg of cable. As he reaches for the dummy, blow the trilling COME. Point your arm down, and he will rush down the second leg to make the delivery.

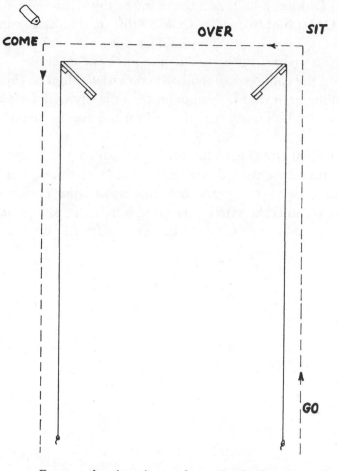

Reverse the situation and practice both ways.

Now place Duke at SIT-STAY and plant a dummy on the other corner. This time, your OVER command will turn him in the opposite direction. Practice back and forth on the U-shaped cable configuration so Duke gets the experience of being sent OVER in both directions as well as BACK and COME, all in the same exercise.

You might want to use dead or harnessed pigeons instead of the dummy to add interest and incentive to handling exercises. At least use a scented dummy to start Duke relying on his nose when being handled.

If the dog begins anticipating where the dummy is and fails to stop for SIT at the corner, drive a U-stake over the cable just around the corner where he should have stopped. And use a choke chain. When the dropper ring hits the stake and jerks Duke to a halt, he'll begin to see the wisdom in accepting your advice to SIT. Order him back with COME whistle, then send him again – and again and again, if necessary. When he does obey SIT, walk to the corner, lift the stake with a crowbar, and send Duke to fetch the dummy.

Try Duke off the cable occasionally so you know when he's ready to accept complete handling in the field. Then practice endlessly with harnessed birds in the field. It's fun. And it's fairly complicated for the dog, so he needs practice to stay competent.

Important: When working in the field, you can stop and turn him, or send him out and bring him around toward you several times, but be sure that without excessive delay you guide him just downwind of the planted bird. Cease handling when Duke starts quartering into the scent, or wagging his tail excitedly. Give no more signals until he reaches for the bird. Then blow the COME trill.

Step 5

Trailing

Duke is now capable of being handled out to any bird you saw fall. But what happens when he gets there? Is the bird dead? Or did it run? Some dogs have good natural trailing instincts, but many won't know what to do with a scent trail if they aren't taught. Furthermore, most retrievers have only average noses. Dr. Larry Myers at Auburn University's Veterinary College devised a way to test scenting ability in dogs, and all indications so far tell us that Labrador retrievers, at least, have just average olfactory powers. It's important, then, to train our retrievers to make best use of what they do have while we hope for breeders to give more emphasis to nose.

Lay the scent trail with the training pole instead of just dragging it.

Start with a wet-feather dummy, or scented dummy, or dunked dead bird. Drag it with a string attached to your training pole so that the bird scent trail will be about 10 feet from yours. Also, try to walk downwind of the drag as you lay the scent. It's important that the dog does not learn he can trail you to find the bird or dummy.

Bring Duke downwind of the trail on leash or check cord, and let him scent-trail and find the dummy.

Let him trail at his own speed.

He'll indicate when he catches the air scent coming from the dummy.

Scott wing straps allow every movement except flying.

Note the concentration required for trailing. Never excite a dog when on trail.

Bring Duke in downwind of the trail. If he doesn't notice the scent by himself, get on your hands and knees and scratch in the grass where the trail starts. He'll wonder what's so interesting. Humans would come in for a look, of course, but being a dog, he'll come in for a sniff. Watch carefully. When you see evidence that he noticed the scent (ears perked, stronger sniffing, slight excitement), urge him to take the trail by saying a quiet FETCH.

Important: There are times while training dogs that it pays to excite them into greater enthusiasm. Trailing is *not* one of those times. Trailing requires great concentration. Other than saying the quiet FETCH, keep your mouth shut. You're only a distraction. If Duke gets off the trail, it's OK to guide him back silently with the check cord, but do *nothing* to excite him. That would only make him run helter-skelter looking for a shortcut instead of patiently working out the puzzle.

If you have a hefty fishing rod, and should Duke wise up to your scent trail always being near the drag, try casting the dummy, then reeling it in to lay a trail. That will leave none of your scent on the trail except what might be on the dummy.

For more complicated scent trails, allow wing-strapped pigeons to walk off through light cover.

When Duke learns to trail the scent drag, make it more difficult by discontinuing the practice of dunking the dummy. When he can trail it dry, he's ready for live birds. Pigeons are best for this, as they're readily available and easy to keep. Use Scott wing straps to prevent the birds from flying. Let them walk out of sight in very thin cover. Then, one by one, let Duke track them down and fetch them back to you.

Persist until Duke is a proficient tracker, then spend that much time again in practice.

Bonus: The scratching in the grass ploy is also a great way to catch a dog that hasn't been trained to, or won't, come when called. They have to be close enough easily to see you scratching, of course, but dogs are often attracted considerable distances by this action. Most trot right in. And because their curiosity compels them to sniff where you're scratching, it's easy to collar them.

Step 6

Force Training

Years ago, I wouldn't force train. We called it force "break" back then, and it sounded worse than it is. But what really shot it down for me was trying it on my first Lab. I pinched his ear, and instead of his mouth flying open in protest, he looked up at me with loving eyes that said, "If you like to pinch my ear, then that's what I like, too." Right then I decided that a dog bred to retrieve shouldn't have to be force trained to retrieve.

Unfortunately, at a later time, and with another dog, I learned that there are indeed occasions when a retriever needs to be force trained to retrieve. One cold morning I had a duck down on the thin ice of a Montana marsh. My dog crashed through. He climbed onto the ice only to fall through again . . . and again . . . and then, thoroughly spooked, he quit. I sent him back. Once more he broke through the ice. This time he quit permanently. The psychological damage wasn't lasting because I was able to jolly him back into retrieving by repeatedly tossing a dead duck a few feet. But I retrieved my own duck out on the ice, and for the rest of the morning I retrieved everybody else's ducks because I was the only one wearing waders.

So there you have it. Make your own choice. Will you force train so your dog knows he *must* fetch, regardless? Or will you fetch your own ducks when the going gets tough?

If it's force train, do it on a bench. Off the ground, with the feeling of unsure footing, dogs have less self-confidence and are quicker to take direction without argument. He may struggle to get off the bench, but hang on. He'll settle down.

Don't begin force training, however, until Duke is far enough along in his training to SIT-STAY with you out of sight. By this point, he is accepting your control well, because experience has taught him that doing what you ask brings fun and praise, not trouble.

Press lips against teeth.

Open Duke's mouth by pressing his upper lips against his teeth.

When the mouth opens to avoid the discomfort, insert the dummy.

A finger under the chin forces the dog to hold the dummy.

As you press on the teeth, say FETCH, and slip the dummy in as the mouth opens. Press a finger under his chin at the point inside the V of his lower jawbones to keep Duke from pushing the dummy out with his tongue. If he doesn't try, relax the finger pressure to test him. If he tries to eject the dummy, use finger pressure again to stop him from opening his mouth. If your dog has been a troublesome dummy dropper, say "Hold it!" as you apply the pressure. If repeated often enough that he learns it, the command can be used to keep the dummy in his mouth when he's trying to drop it short of delivering to hand.

Duke probably enjoys holding the dummy in his mouth well enough not to fight this, but some dogs do. After he settles down, or after a few moments of holding it, say GIVE, and take the dummy.

Practice the whole sequence over and over until the dog is willing to stand with the dummy until told GIVE.

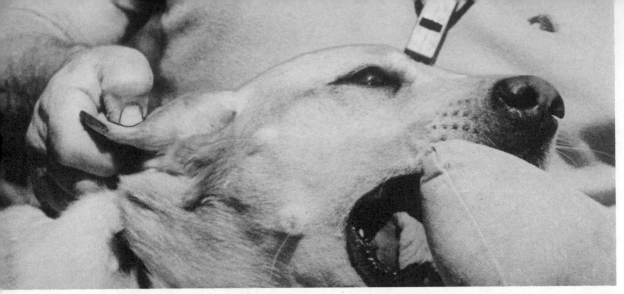

The ear pinch is the heart of force training.

Duke knows what you want by this time. Now he must open his own mouth to accept the dummy. Place the fingers of your left hand under his collar. Position his ear between the collar and your thumb. Now pinch with your thumbnail as you say FETCH. The instant Duke opens his mouth to protest, slide the dummy inside, and release the ear pinch. After a few times (more or less, depending upon the dog's intelligence) he'll learn that the pain ends when he opens his mouth. He'll become quick about it to avoid the pinch. Make sure that you do release the pinch exactly when Duke's mouth opens.

For stubborn dogs, a beer tab enhances the ear pinch.

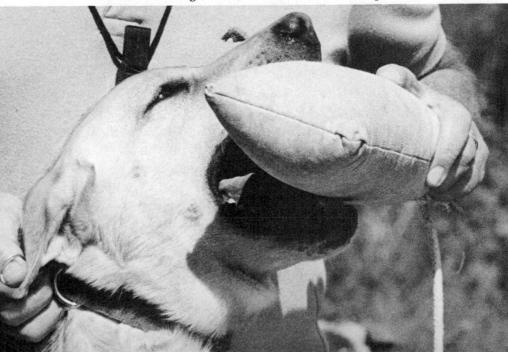

Some dogs with high pain thresholds, and/or stubborn natures, can be very resistant to opening their mouths on demand. They may not respond until a tender spot develops on the ear. Arizona trainer, Bruce Ludwig, showed me how to use a beer can tab to speed the process with such dogs. The tab concentrates the force in a narrower line than does a thumb and nail.

When Duke starts taking the dummy to avoid the pinch, make him reach for it.

Next place the dummy on the bench, and as you practice, move it farther and farther away.

When Duke is consistently opening his mouth to accept the dummy, and doing it quickly to avoid the pinch, stop putting the dummy in his mouth. Hold it an inch from his face, and make him take it himself. When he catches on, make him reach farther and farther to get it. Next, place the dummy on the bench. If Duke has trouble with this, touch it with a finger. You've been holding the dummy until now, and that has become a visual clue. When he's picking it up, gradually move it farther and farther away on the bench as you practice.

When the dog will consistently take perhaps three steps to grab the dummy, he has grasped that refusing is not an option when he hears the word FETCH. And, when out in the field or blind, his ear is always handy if he needs a reminder.

Step 7

Fetch Cripple First

Question: You've just dropped two ducks with two shots. Great shooting. But one duck did flutter down. Which will Duke retrieve first?

Answer: Probably the last to fall because it's easiest to remember. And chances are 50-50 that the first one fluttered down, and that the duck is now swimming away while Duke's delivering the one that couldn't go anywhere, anyhow.

The answer to the question *you're* about to ask is, yes, there is a way to train Duke to go for the cripple first.

This is another of Mayo Kellogg's "magic methods." I love 'em. They sometimes border on being "Rube Goldberg" inventions, but they work.

Mayo uses three pigeons. A large fishing weight is tied to the foot of one. Unfortunately, I can't tell you exactly how heavy the weight should be, because pigeons vary in size and strength. You need just enough so the bird is pulled down fluttering when he's thrown. Buy some large weights, tie more than enough on one foot (with yarn; it doesn't cut the leg), and toss the bird. Remove one weight at a time until the bird can flutter a short distance, but can't sustain flight.

Launch the birds together like a covey rise.

The other two birds can be thrown by a helper, or helpers, but Mayo uses a bird-release cage. It doesn't matter—just so all three birds are launched at the same time. One of the two unweighted birds will be shot. The other will fly back to the loft. All of this is quite like a covey rise. One escapes, one is shot, another appears crippled.

The dog will go to the fluttering bird first and thus learn to give priority to the crippled bird.

If you have Duke steady to flush and/or shot by this time, send him to make the retrieve immediately after the shot so that, hopefully, the fluttering bird will still be making a commotion. If Duke's not steady, you'll let him go with the birds. Either way, have him on a check cord so you can stop him if he goes toward the dead bird first. He'll then see the live bird and fetch it. Almost always, he'll retrieve the fluttering bird first, anyway, because it's closer and its movement is attention-getting. Then send him for the dead bird.

It doesn't take many practice sessions to accustom the dog to fetching the cripple first. As soon as he's consistent, count the birds he has fetched, and give him that many more to establish the habit.

If you're short of birds, there's no need to kill more. Freeze the dead bird, but thaw it before each session. Have a helper throw it and release the live bird at the same time. Shoot before the dead bird falls. And quickly, about the time you shoot, the helper should be throwing the weighted bird.

If you're reusing the dead bird, you may want to vary the throw sequence to give Duke a variety such as he may encounter in the field. Throw the weighted bird first. Shoot, but miss. Or throw the live bird first and miss. Mix it up. But always insist that Duke fetch the fluttering bird first.

Step 8

Cripple First in Water

Duke already retrieves cripples first on land. And he has already fetched wing-tethered ducks in water. Chances are, he'll go for cripples first on water without further training. But if you want to be sure, work with a dummy on a string.

As Duke approaches the three dummies, jiggle the center one with the string to get the dog's attention.

Throw three dummies about six feet apart on the water. The center dummy will have the string attached. As Duke gets near the group, jiggle the center dummy with the string to get his attention. Pull it a little to make it swim. The instant Duke notices it, say FETCH. Whistle the double tweet for emphasis. If he doesn't switch, pull the dummy faster. Then slow down so he can catch it.

Send the dog for the other two dummies.

Practice until he looks for a moving decoy, then practice that long again.

Step 9

Diving Dog

Wing-crippled ducks can drive a dog insane. Every time he gets close, the duck dives. Maybe the dog sees it surface again. And maybe he chases it around until it dives time after time and finally comes up among the cattails where he never sees it again. Or perhaps it's a seriously wounded duck that dives to the bottom and dies with its bill in a death hold on a tree root or weed stem. Our dog needs to dive underwater after these ducks.

Search-and-rescue dogs have proved that canines are capable of finding people by "smelling" underwater. Actually, they are recognizing scent by its taste in the water, which isn't much different from odor. Retrievers that somehow learn they can dive have often astounded humans by their uncanny ability to find ducks under water so muddy that a webbed foot couldn't be seen two inches from the eyes. We know they're doing more than stumbling upon the duck underwater, and we know that this is a highly desirable thing for a retriever to be capable of doing; *but,* how in the world do we train a dog to do this?!

Believe it or not, it's easy. And it will probably come as no surprise that I found the quickest method in Mayo Kellogg's bag of tricks.

206

Diving dog training equipment.

    Mayo's equipment is simple: a floating dummy, a length of 125-pound-test nylon cord, and a heavy iron of roughly mushroom-anchor shape with an eye welded to the upright member.

With the string passing through the sunken weight, Mayo Kellogg throws the dummy.

The equipment's use is equally simple. The cord passes through the eye of the weight which is sunk in two or three feet of water. Mayo holds one end of the cord. The other end is attached to the dummy. By now, of course, Duke is both swimming and fetching with enthusiasm, so that's no problem. We follow Mayo's example and step back a few feet from the weight, throw the dummy, and have Duke fetch it, being careful that he has enough slack string to make the delivery.

Just as the dog is about to grab, sink the dummy just beneath the surface.

Duke will sink his nose to keep the dummy from escaping.

The next time, we pull in the slack string after the throw, send Duke, and just as he starts to reach for the dummy, we pull it barely beneath the surface. Our dog will see it disappearing and make a quick grab, getting no more than his nose underwater.

This time Duke is coming up after being totally submerged while diving for the dummy.

Gradually, very gradually, we pull the dummy just a little deeper with each retrieve until Duke is actually diving completely underwater to get it.

The dog may tangle with the string — you might too — but persist. It works.

When the dog is becoming good at diving, we can start backing away from the sunken weight (never farther than half the length of our cord, of course) to make longer retrieves. You might tangle a time or two — Duke may also — but persist. It won't take long before Duke will be amazing your hunting friends with his diving retrieves.

Step 10

Coup de Grace — Circling

If you think your friends were amazed by Duke's diving retrieves, wait until they see this. Picture yourself hunting pheasants. You're moving through a strip of good bird cover, and your dog is searching beautifully and within proper range, but the cocks are running far to the front. Opening day was three weeks ago, and hunting pressure has already given them a college education. A buddy has the gall to suggest that he circle to the end of the cover and block — that is, get all the shooting when the birds run out the other end. Your other buddies are too polite to suggest that you and Duke just act as pushers, so they quietly wait for your response.

"Naw," you say, "let's all be end shooters and let Duke do the pushing."

In most circles, that ought to bring dumbfounded looks all around. Only a very small percentage of dogs have ever been smart enough to learn that they can circle birds and herd them back to the hunters. It was also generally conceded among trainers that this was something they could not teach dogs to do. As a result, very few hunters even know it can be done. But just between you and me, if you've trained Duke through *Part 2, Step 4*, he already knows how.

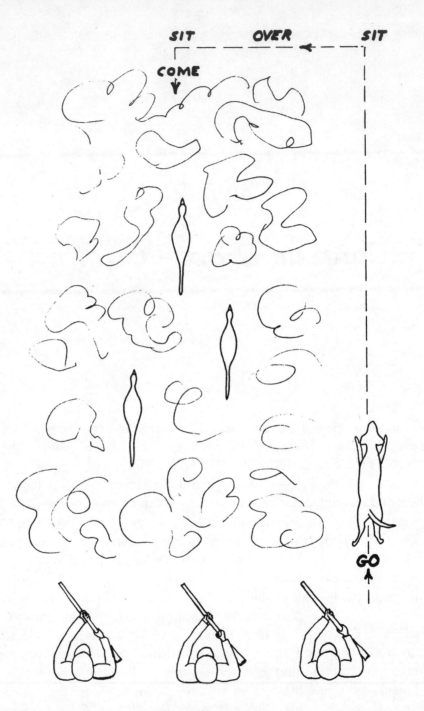

The retriever that has been taught to handle can be guided into circling running birds. After a few times, many learn to do it without guidance.

Take Duke outside the cover's edge about 20 feet, if there's that much space available. Send him with the whistle on a line paralleling the edge of the cover. If he tries to turn back into the cover to resume hunting, SIT him with the whistle. When he looks back for direction, whistle the double tweet to send him again, and raise your arm to signal BACK. Persist with Duke until you get him all the way to the end of the cover.

SIT him again, then send him with whistle and arm signals for OVER to about the middle of the cover strip. Blow SIT again. This time trill for COME. Maybe Duke will dash through the cover to get back. If he happens to be running into the wind, he'll probably quarter back. And maybe he'll recognize the opportunity and actually hunt all the way back.

Understand, of course, to accomplish this, Duke must handle 100 to 200 yards out. But once he has done it a few times, if he's intelligent, you won't have to work him down to the other end. He'll catch on fast after he sees you shoot a few of the birds he has driven back. Very likely, he'll start circling birds on his own. But if he isn't this intelligent, and if he never does understand what he's doing, who cares as long as he takes the hand signals and pushes the pheasants?

This same trick works as well in ditches, drywashes, and along stream edges as it does in cover strips. It also works with Western quail, most of which can be running fools when the cover is sparse, and/or they're educated. Regardless whether the dog does it intelligently or mechanically, just doing it can really rescue a potentially lost hunt.

Step 11

Ready for Season

If you have persevered in the Speed-Train System, you now have an outstanding dog. Opening day approaches. How hard will you hunt? A duck, or two, or three, to fetch? Or will you hunt upland birds all day, expecting Duke to quarter continually ahead as well as retrieve game? Or have you even planned a week's vacation in which you'll hunt ducks early and upland birds the remainder of the day?

Think about what you're asking your dog to do. And make sure he's physically prepared. If it's just a few fetches, he's ready. If the exercise will be extreme, he's not. In that case, consider roading him. It's simple. You drive the car; he runs alongside on a 8-foot cord. Don't try to run with him. Even if you're a jogger, you're too slow to make it real exercise for the dog.

Look for a seldom-used road. Drive with the right hand, hold the long leash or cord in your left hand, and never cease being aware of both the road ahead and your dog alongside. When Duke gets the urge to relieve himself, he *will not* ask to stop at the next gas station. He'll squat without warning. If you aren't prepared either to stop or let go, you'll find out which is grown on tightest—his head or your arm. If you see a vehicle approaching from front or behind, stop early, and bring Duke safely to the side of your car while you wait for the other auto to pass.

Running along while you jog is no exercise for the dog. Road him at a lope for three miles a day, and he'll be in condition for nearly anything he encounters during hunting season.

There aren't many dirt roads left over much of the country, and surfaced roads are hard on feet, so start doing one-half mile each day and build up gradually. Blacktop can be very hot to bare feet and very abrasive as well, so try to pick a cool time of day.

Drive at a speed that makes your dog lope to keep up—not a trot or lazy lope as a dog might do running beside a jogger, and not flat out running as hard as he can go, but a lope that just puts a little pressure on the dog to keep up.

Watch his pads. They should toughen. If they're wearing and becoming sore, cease roading, and let them heal. Build toughness gradually. Once the pads can take it, roading three miles a day will condition a dog for most hunting.

If Duke is not in top condition when the time comes to hunt days in a row, all is not lost. Endurance can be improved by using vitamin C. It has been proven in sled-dog tests, and I proved it with beagles. I use vitamin C myself. It increases endurance by greatly reducing muscle soreness caused when an unconditioned body engages in extreme exercise.

It's important that the dog has extra vitamin C in his body when the hunt starts, so pop some down his throat as you load him. Excess C goes out with the urine, so give him more when you take the noon break. And give him another dose when you retire him for the night.

Understand that we're not dealing with "minimum daily requirements" here, but rather a strong and steady wash of C in the blood, which is necessary to make a constant supply of collagen to build back, cell by cell, the microscopic muscle tears that are felt as soreness. I can only say that I know 12 grams a day in 3-gram doses about every four hours works great for me at about 175 pounds. From this, I calculated 500 mg three times a day for beagles, and they did well. I give a 50 to 60-pound dog four grams (eight 500 mg tablets) administered either two tablets four times a day or three before hunting, two at the break, and three after the hunt.

Step 12

Going Backward

I've noticed that when dogs change hands, it usually happens around two years of age. The owner will sometimes confide in you, saying, "He seemed to have it all as a pup. Then he started going backward. He can't remember his training— or doesn't want to. Acts contrary. Something ruined him, but I can't figure out what it was."

Something ruined him all right. But hang on. It's only temporary. He tried you at puberty (11 to 14 months) and now, at 22 to 24 months, he's making his most serious bid for control over his life and those around him. The problem is almost always worse with males than females. My rule of thumb is that if they showed lots of early promise, and if they are handled carefully at these times, they'll come back at least as good and often better when they mature past this stage. If they show little promise during puppyhood, I give them away as pets long before two years of age.

Time alone can cure much of this problem. But what remains of it, if not corrected, can make you just want to be rid of the dog. In most cases, the dogs are uncooperative and do what they want. In extreme cases, males become dangerously possessive about female owners, whom they often try to dominate. They may snap at, or even bite, male owners they do not fear.

The basic reason? Dogs are dogs, and people are people. There are enough similarities to develop wonderful rapport between the two species. But the differences, if not understood and dealt with, can make you hate man's best friend.

For example, women have great faith in words. Offending dogs hear lots of them. But although dogs can learn to understand a few words, long strings are meaningless to them, and are tuned out—especially after the first couple of times that the threatening tone is not followed by punishment after all. Obviously, women behaving as described are expecting dogs to react as humans have reacted to their words. Instead, dogs are genetically programmed to react as dogs, and words are not a part of their communications. In addition, yappy, whiny voice tones are puppylike and inspire further disrespect.

Men have great faith in force. A show of impatience is followed by hit, kick, or whip, and a confident, "There! He won't try that again." For whatever it means, and I'm not at all sure it's flattering, male behavior does more nearly parallel that of dogs. Dogs do understand force. They depend largely on clear dominance signals, but persistent offenders do get thrashed by other dogs that are accustomed to being in control.

Unfortunately, there's a big difference between human force and canine control. When we don't understand this difference, our use of force, to a dog, is like a short circuit, a bolt of lightning that comes at him without warning. He sees us as unstable, unpredictable—and those words come to describe our relationship with the dog as well.

In a functioning pack, canines do not just suddenly attack one another to see who will exercise control. You discovered some of how they do behave in *Part 1, Step 9* when you learned how to become "Top Dog." As animal behaviorist Steve Rafe points out, dogs have ritualistic tests to help decide who is in control. The top dog puts a leg or head over the neck of a subordinate dog. He grasps the muzzle of the dog he wants to control. If the contest becomes more serious, he'll have the subordinate dog on the ground, and will hold him down, perhaps growling. All of these things should be done by us to establish control over Duke if, and whenever, necessary. They are the moves that canines understand. Most important, when control is established by these moves, the dog accepts his position, and respects us as top dog. In contrast, a sudden beating only inspires fear and suspicion. For more details on this, contact Steve Rafe about current publications. His address is listed in the appendix.

All right, you say, but what about the top dog in a canine pack that does finally attack, and attempt to defeat, a subordinate dog that's testing him? It

If the contest becomes serious, put the dog on the ground, lay on him, grip his entire muzzle, and shake it as you threaten vocally.

rarely goes that far, but sometimes a young dog is aggressive enough, and serious enough, to persist until control is won or lost in a fight. It's even less likely to happen between you and your dog.

Steve Rafe believes that neotony makes the difference. Neotony is the retention of infantile characteristics. Over many centuries, we have selected dogs for such things as puppy-like flop ears and high-domed heads. It's less obvious in behavior, but it's there nevertheless, Steve says. And these desirable immature behavior characteristics can be reinforced to help control the dog.

Puppies, for example, especially among wild canines (but the instinct remains among domestic dogs), receive regurgitated food from their parents. The scent and flavor of saliva in food is then connected with parental authority, subordination to that parent, the expectation of good things from the parent figure, and overall, whatever emotions that the "me Pup, you Pop" responses to saliva might conjure up.

Old-time hunters let dogs lick spittle from their hands when they had nothing else handy to offer as a reward, and it worked well. Steve Rafe, in a

When the dog relaxes submissively, hold the position for a moment longer, but be silent. Then release with praise.

more scientific manner, has proven to his own satisfaction, and that of a great many clients, that spitting in a dog's food daily will greatly help control dogs by reinforcing their feeling of "me Pup, you Pop." It is certainly worth a try on that difficult dog.

The major element in canine control is something you may not be quite prepared for. Once again, dogs are dogs, not little people. People don't urinate to establish control over territory or other members of the pack, advertise sexual readiness, express fear (well, maybe we've done that), or convey a variety of other messages. One pointer watched a guest miss 14 quail in a row, then trotted up to the man, cocked his leg, and filled the fellow's boot. The dog's message was well taken, and the man settled down to hit three quail in a row. One dog urinated on its invalid kennel-mate when human strangers came to see them. He feared that a stranger might take his pal, so he urinated on the subordinate dog to show protectiveness.

It's both the dominance and protective qualities of urination that Steve Rafe recognizes as very instrumental in controlling difficult dogs. Obviously, this is not a socially acceptable training method, but a specimen in a squirt bottle is every bit as effective as the real thing. Once a day for three or more days will usually bring that dog under control in a canine-acceptable manner that leaves the dog both happy and willing to cooperate.

Almost always, the dog can be brought under control without beating. I'm not trying to make you a nicey-nice bleeding heart, because I'm not one myself. But I can tell you that beatings cause problems that take time to correct. Try every way possible to avoid them if you want to Speed-Train.

This is the most important move in dog training. The author gives his dog an ATTABOY!

Appendix

Equipment

Pigeon harnesses, Bob West feather dummy, and training cable
T.E. Scott Co.
10329 Rockville Rd.
Indianapolis, IN 46234.
Phone: 317-271-2482.

Underwater dummy release plans
Mayo E. Kellogg
RR3, Box 120
Madison, SD 57042.
Phone: 605-256-3496.

Dog behavior publications
Steve Rafe, Starfire Enterprises
PO Box 4509
Warren, NJ 07060.
Phone: 201-755-2233.

Clay-bird trap to launch Bob West dummies
Penguin Industries, Inc.
Airport Industrial Mall
Coatesville, PA 19320.
Phone: 215-384-6000.